Exploring

SOUTH CAROLINA
STATE PARKS

Exploring
SOUTH CAROLINA
STATE PARKS

A Guide to the State Parks in South Carolina

J.L. and Lin Stepp

Mountain Hill Press

A Division of S & S Communications

Exploring South Carolina State Parks
Copyright©2021
James L. Stepp

Cover Design by Katherine E. Stepp
Cover Photos by J.L. and Lin Stepp
Book Design and Layout by Mountain Hill Press
Editorial Assistance by Elizabeth S. James
Interior Photos by J.L and Lin Stepp

Published by Mountain Hill Press
A division of S & S Communications

Author note. This is a non-fiction guidebook created by the authors based on their visitations and research of South Carolina State Parks. Effort has been made to ensure accuracy of specific environs and place names, but places and names may change over time as do descriptive trail details.

Library of Congress Cataloging-in-Publication Data

Stepp, J.L. and Lin
    Exploring South Carolina State Parks: A Guide to the State Parks in South Carolina
    by J.L. and Lin Stepp
    ISBN 978-1-7361643-8-9
    eISBN 978-1-7361643-9-6

Non-Fiction. 1. State Parks—South Carolina—Guidebooks. 2. Parks—Southeast—Guide books. 3. Travel—South Carolina—Guidebooks.
    I. Stepp, J.L. and Lin II. Title
    Library of Congress Control Number: 2021901847

ACKNOWLEDGMENTS

Thanks and gratitude goes to the South Carolina Department of Parks, Recreation and Tourism located in Columbia, South Carolina. We are deeply grateful for:
- their mission to manage, protect, and preserve scenic areas;
- their fine state park website detailing each of the forty-seven state parks, which helped us with the accuracy of our book;
- their careful and meticulous care in designing and maintaining all the parks throughout the state of South Carolina, making each a pleasure to visit.

Additional thanks goes to the South Carolina branch of the National Park Service, located in Washington DC, for:
- their part in managing, protecting and preserving scenic areas not only in South Carolina but around the US;
- their efforts to preserve and maintain unique historic and natural sites in the state that we enjoyed visiting and including in this guidebook;

Appreciation and thanks also goes to:
- the park rangers and visitor center staff in each park we visited who answered questions and helped us with information at our park visits;

Thanks also to Kim and Sean Peterson who shared some of their SC Wyndham resort time with us so we could finish our book at a nice location on Lake Marion.

A special acknowledgement goes to Drew Tapp, the Community Relations Manager (CRM) at the Barnes & Noble, in Westwood Plaza, 1812 Sam Rittenberg Blvd, in Charleston, South Carolina, who pushed and encouraged us in 2019 to write this book while we were at the store for a scheduled Book Signing for Lin's South Carolina novel *Claire At Edisto*. If Drew hadn't pushed on us to create this guidebook, it might not have happened.

Discovering
TENNESSEE
STATE PARKS

A Guide to the State Parks in Tennessee
J.L. and Lin Stepp

THE *Afternoon*
HIKER
A GUIDE TO CASUAL HIKES IN THE
GREAT SMOKY MOUNTAINS

J.L. AND LIN STEPP

Introduction

Our journey of writing guidebooks began hiking in the Great Smoky Mountains Park near our home. We'd always visited in the park with our kids, but now, with an empty nest and more leisure time, we discovered hiking in a new way. The trail guides we purchased seemed geared to more veteran hikers than us, provided often unclear directions to the trailheads, and information we really didn't need. So we decided to write our own guidebook suitable for non-Sierra types like ourselves, looking for easily accessible, enjoyable hikes that could be completed in an afternoon. *The Afternoon Hiker*, published in 2014, was the result, describing 110 trails in the Smoky Mountains with color photos throughout.

A U.S. Government shut down in 2014 of all the national parks, including the Smokies, led us to check out state parks as an alternative hiking option for our weekend getaways. After not finding any guidebooks with the park-by-park descriptions we hoped for, we decided to write our own. Over the next two years we visited all 56 of the state parks in Tennessee creating a guidebook similar in format to our hiking guide. The book, *Discovering Tennessee State Parks*, published in 2018, provides directions to and descriptions of every park in Tennessee with over 700 color photos in illustration.

In 2019 while vacationing in South Carolina at Edisto Beach and doing bookstore signings around the area for Lin's latest novel, set at Edisto, many of our fans and readers—and several individuals in the bookstores where we had scheduled events—encouraged us to consider writing a similar parks guidebook for South Carolina. After a little thought we decided to do so and started a new adventure visiting and exploring parks around the state. The first state park we visited was at Edisto where we have vacationed every year since the 1980s. The second was at Hunting Island State Park below Beaufort. Through 2019 and 2020, we visited all 47 of the state parks in the four regions of the state, the Upstate, Midlands, Pee Dee, and Lowcountry areas. Because we found many interesting historic sites and parks around South Carolina, managed by the National Parks system versus the state, we chose to also add eight National Parks and historic sites to this guidebook, bringing the total of parks visited to 55.

The resulting book, *Exploring South Carolina State Parks,* records the journey of our park visits. It's the perfect travel companion for those wanting to visit and explore any or all of South Carolina's parks. With each park visited, we included directions to get to the site, a description of the park, its sections and amenities, trails to hike, things to do and see, and the month of the year we visited—since different seasons offer different pleasures in the parks. In addition, we included hundreds of color photos throughout the book of special scenes in every park to give readers a flavor of what they might see at their visits. We hope you will use and cherish this book as you tour and enjoy the incredible variety of parks scattered across the state of South Carolina.

If you plan to visit many—or all—of South Carolina's state parks, pick up *The Official Guide to South Carolina State Parks* book, free at a park office or order it online at the parks website: southcarolinaparks.com. Collect a stamp for each park you visit and when you complete collecting all the stamps you can get the official "I Visited All 47 State Parks" T-shirt.

TABLE OF CONTENTS

HISTORY OF STATE PARKS

The history of the state and national parks are intertwined. State parks, like national ones, were established to preserve locations of natural beauty and recreational potential and to safeguard places of historic significance. The first national park, Yellowstone National Park, was established by an Act of Congress in 1872 and signed by President Ulysses Grant, beginning the national parks movement. More parks followed, especially out west, before Southern ones began to develop. President Theodore Roosevelt was a great champion in advancing the national park movement, and many bird and game preserves, national forests, parks, and monuments were established during his presidency.

The first state park was Niagara Falls State Park, established in 1885, with a few others following in the late 1800s and early 1900s. In 1921, at the request of Stephen Mather, National Park Service Director, a group of preservationists and conservationists met in Iowa to discuss the concept of developing additional parks at the state level. This 1921 National Conference of State Parks, hosted by the National Park Service, spurred interest in developing more sites around America and initiated the state park movement. At the time of the conference twenty-nine states, including South Carolina, had no parks, but by 1925, all forty-eight states had begun to formulate development plans. Although the beginning of the Depression slowed growth, many recreational areas were developed later in the 1930s through Depression-era programs like the Civilian Conservation Corps (CCC) and the Works Progress Administration (WPA). States around the U.S. recognized that lands needed to be preserved at the local level that would not become designated as national sites. By 1972, every state in the U.S. had a state parks system.

In South Carolina, as in other states, federal involvement and local initiatives led to the development of parks around the state. South Carolina's state parks, like others in America were created to preserve and protect unique recreational, historic, cultural, and scenic natural areas. Although work on several parks began around the same time, Cheraw State Park, was the first to be developed in 1934 in the Pee Dee area of the state. Soon other parks, sixteen in total, were developed within six years by the CCC around the state, with Myrtle Beach State Park the first to officially open to the public on July 1, 1936. Other parks were developed through governmental and state agencies like the US Forest Service.

Improved roads, better transportation, and more interest in travel as a leisure activity began to make the state parks in South Carolina, and other states, more desirable destinations in the 1940s following the war years. The economic state around the nation had improved, too, and the state and nation responded by developing more parks and by improving existing parks with more amenities and facilities. Campgrounds were developed and expanded, many cabins built, swimming pools, pavilions, and picnic areas were constructed and more access to lakes via fishing piers and boat ramps. More trained rangers began to be hired in every park and educational and natural environmental programs developed.

By the 1970s, all these improvements and expansions, had resulted in budget problems, and to assist with this problem the state instituted entrance fees at many of their parks. Today, most all parks in South Carolina have an entrance fee, or a yearly pass and car tag can be purchased to allow year-round entrance to all the state parks. Also in South Carolina, most park offices are only open for limited hours in each day, generally from 11:00 am to 12:00 pm and from 4:00 pm to 5:00 pm. In planning a visit to South Carolina parks be aware of the admissions fees and park office hours in advance.

There are, at the time of this guidebook's publication, forty-seven state parks in South Carolina managed by the South Carolina Department of Parks, Recreation and Tourism, their main office located in Columbia, SC [Website at: www.south-carolinaparks.com]. Additionally, in South Carolina many natural areas, military parks, historic sites, and battlefields are managed by the National Park Service. Because many of these sites are located near the state parks and are also interesting to explore and visit, we chose to include eight parks maintained by the National Park Service in our guidebook. South Carolina National Park Service sites are managed and operated by a staff of National Park Service employees at the different South Carolina park locations and by the National Park Service, U.S. Department of the Interior, Washington, DC. [Website: www.nps.gov]

Throughout the U.S., and in South Carolina, state parks are a treasure often unappreciated or applauded. They give Americans a place to get out-of-doors for recreation and pleasure in locales close to their homes. The scenic areas benefit individuals by creating opportunities for family bonding, relieving stress, and providing peaceful time in nature. Parks provide economic and ecological value and conserve environmental and historic riches that might otherwise have been lost. They serve as a catalyst for tourism, provide activities for youth leisure, offer recreational venues for groups, and are a rich source of pride for individual states and their communities. Franklin D. Roosevelt wrote: "The nation that destroys its soil, destroys itself" and many other leaders have realized the value of conserving lands and waters for future generations. South Carolina's state parks offer opportunity for all its citizens to enjoy time out of doors in beautiful locations.

"Earth and sky, woods and fields, lakes and river, the mountains and the sea, are excellent school masters, and teach of us more than we can ever learn from books." – John Lubbock

Caesars Head

UPSTATE SOUTH CAROLINA STATE PARK INDEX

UPSTATE
South Carolina
PARKS

Oconee

Keowee-Toxaway

Musgrove Mill

Ninety Six

Jones Gap State Park

Upstate - Greenville County
Park Address: 303 Jones Gap Road, Marietta, SC 29661
Park Size: 4,246 Acres   Month Visited: September
Directions: From the north via Hwy 25 or from the south via Hwy 276, turn on Hwy 11 (Geer Highway) to brown park sign at River Falls Rd; follow River Falls Rd for 9 miles, approximately 15 minutes, to park entrance.

Park Description:

Park Description:
  Jones Gap State Park lies in the far northwest corner of South Carolina. It sits along the border of the Mountain Bridge Wilderness Area in a 13,000-acre forested wilderness on the Blue Ridge Escarpment that bridges the Table Rock and Poinsett watersheds. This is a beautiful backcountry park, home to 600 types of wildflowers, 160 songbirds, and 60 varieties of mammals. It is known mainly for its outdoor beauty and over 60 miles of hiking trails, many with waterfalls. The Middle Saluda River, running through the park, was the first river designated a scenic river in South Carolina.
  The park, despite its beauty and popularity, has limited parking allowing only 37 vehicles at a time, so visitors who arrive at busy tourist seasons or

on weekends may wait up to an hour or more to get into this recreation area. After parking, a winding trail leads through the woods, across a wooden bridge spanning over the river, and into the main park. One of the first sights you see as you near the visitor center is the spillway dam behind the Cleveland Fish Hatchery. Beyond the spillway is the restored fish hatchery pond, built in 1931 to try to preserve the diminishing trout

population. The hatchery operated for over 30 years until closing in 1963. It was later restored and restocked with mountain brook and rainbow trout— creating a pretty sight to walk around and see with kiosks explaining the hatchery's history.

Below the hatchery on the river are picnic tables and a pavilion and on the hillside above the hatchery is the park visitor center. The visitor center contains a large meeting room where educational programs are often held and visitors can purchase a hiking trail map or other maps and items in the office. The two most popular trails for general visitors to the park are the Jones Gap Falls Trail and the Rainbow Falls Trail. Both begin at the same trailhead to the right after crossing a wooden bridge beyond the visitor center. Both trails are rocky and rough with uneven terrain, often steep, and might be difficult for some individuals to hike.

However, anyone can easily hike a short distance up the broad Jones Gap Trail to enjoy scenic spots along the cascading river even if they don't walk the entire 1.5 miles [or 3 miles RT] to the falls. The hike on to

Jones Gap Falls continues along the stream, following blue blazes marking the way, crossing a few footbridges, and passing several backcountry campsites. In early summer the mountain laurel is very pretty along the trailside. After a moderately difficult uphill climb, around rocks and boulders in the pathway, the trail comes to the wooden Reid Clonts Memorial Bridge at about one mile. After walking over the wooden bridge, the trail moves on to soon cross a tributary over stepping stones just past Campsite #11. Watch for a park sign after the campsite and follow the spur trail beside it a short distance to the falls. Here Jones Gap Falls cascades for 50-feet down a granite bluff into a large pool. Big boulders around the pool provide a nice spot to rest and enjoy the falls before turning to return or continuing further on up the 5.3-miles trail deeper into the Mountain Bridge Wilderness area.

To hike to Rainbow Falls instead, watch for an intersection and trail sign at 0.75-miles up the Jones Gap Trail. Turn right on this red-blazed trail to continue. The first part of the hike is pleasant, crossing several bridges. The trail then begins climbing 1000 ft in a steep upward trek, passing a stone bridge and climbing a set of rocky stairs before reaching the Rainbow Falls, a 100-foot plume that drops over a tall rocky face. The cascade is stunning when full, dropping into a pool and then spilling over the rocks below in more cascades, but in dry weather, after scant rainfall, the falls may be only a thin rivulet spurting over the bluffs and hardly worth a photograph. The rocks and boulders around the falls are mossy and slippery, so be watchful. Many people fall and get hurt here every year. The 2.3-miles [6.4 miles RT] hike to Rainbow Falls is a longer and much more strenuous one than the easier hike to Jones Gap Falls but leads to a high and impressive waterfall.

Many other hiking trails wander out of the park, some connecting over to Caesars Head State Park on the other side of the Mountain Bridge Wilderness Area, like the 4.3-miles Rim of the Gap Trail near the visitor center. Across the road 4.9- miles Hospital Rock Trail begins. We hiked a little of the Hospital Rock Trail, nice and easy underfoot in its beginnings, and following a forested landscape before growing difficult, steep and treacherous as it climbs up Standingstone Mountain. At about two miles, the trail leads to the house-sized boulder of Hospital Rock with a cave under it, where Confederate soldiers hid during the Civil War, and to 100-foot Falls Creek Falls near its end.

This is a beautiful park to visit, especially for hiking enthusiasts and those who love to fish for trout in the mountain streams. The park also has many backcountry campsites including several near the visitor center area. If possible, visit off-season or on a weekday to gain a parking space without needing to wait. You'll make memories.

History Note:
This park, and Jones Gap Falls and trail, were named for Solomon Jones (1802-1899). Jones, a self-taught mountain road builder, built a road from this wilderness area across the mountains to Cedar Mountain, North Carolina. Local stories about Jones say he blazed the trail starting in the 1840s following the lead of a big sow hog and using mainly a hatchet. When the unpaved road was complete, it was the only route between Greenville County in South Carolina and Transylvania County, North Carolina, and Jones took tolls to allow travelers to use it until the 1930s when the Geer Highway was built.

Caesars Head State Park

Upstate - Greenville Conty
Park Address: 8155 Geer Highway, Cleveland, SC 29635
Park Size: 7,467 Acres   Month Visited: September
Directions: From the north via Hwy 25 or from south via Hwy 276, travel on
merged Hwy 276 and Hwy 11, continuing to brown park sign and follow road 7
miles into park.

Park Description:

Caesars Head State Park lies
at the other end of the Mountain Bridge
Wilderness Area, not far from nearby
Jones Gap State Park, with hiking trails
latticing between the two. Caesars Head,
the larger park, lies on the boundary of
Transylvania County, North Carolina,
and has 60 miles of challenging hiking
trails,18 primitive campsites, and several
impressive waterfalls. In the spring the
park is on the songbird migration route
and from September to November thousands of hawks migrate through the park.

The visitor center at Caesars
Head is the first place to stop when entering the park. It's a large one with a
gift shop, books, and area information.
There are shaded picnic tables near the
visitors center, many with fine views, at
this high point on top of the mountain.
From the parking lot follow the sidewalk
to the Caesar's Head Overlook Trail. It's
a short 0.3-miles trail, mostly along a
wooden walkway, to stupendous views.
The trail actually walks right out onto
the rocky precipice, Caesars Head, that
the park is named for—a fine place for
photo shoots and oohing and aahing over
the spectacular views. Around on a side
trail you can see the rocky cliff from a
lower angle and see the head shape that gave the rock and park its name. Climb
over the rocks behind the overlook to also see the Devil's Kitchen. A sign on the
fence directs you to a long staircase climbing down into a narrow crevice in the
18

huge granite rocks piled there. Old legends say the devil made this crevice by pouring hot liquid into this crack. At the bottom of the stairs, a short rocky trail walks under the rocks to come out on the other side to another railed walkway with wonderful views. This was our favorite area in the park and worth the visit by itself.

The rest of the park is a hiking and fishing paradise. We checked out several of the trails, walking all of a few and portions of others. Directly across from the visitor center parking lot is a moderately difficult trail most could hike and enjoy, the 1.9-miles Frank Coggins Trail. It drops downhill on a narrow trail through the woods to loop around and then return. At about one fourth mile the trail passes the Coldspring Connector Trail and then continues to a "T" where the trail loops both left and right. Following the loop to the left, counter clockwise, the trail passes two waterfalls along the way, both pretty if the mountains haven't been too dry. Cliff Falls is first at appx 0.8 mile where the creek cascades 20-25 feet down a small rocky cliff. Further around the loop is Firewater Falls, a long 75 ft. narrow spill over a giant rock, with a little cave area below it. Midway around the loop, the path passes the beginning of the Naturaland Trust Trail, a long, strenuous, and challenging 5.8-miles trail which ends a short distance after a long suspension bridge near Raven Cliff Falls.

Driving on down the road a mile from the visitor center leads to a parking lot where three other trailheads begin, the Tom Miller Trail, the

Coldspring Branch Trail and across the street the popular Raven Cliff Falls Trail. The blue-blazed 0.7-miles Tom Miller Trail is a short strenuous connector trail that links to Jones Gap Trail. The orange-blazed Coldspring Branch Trail, 2.3 miles (4.6 miles RT), also leads over to the Jones Gap park. This trail wanders downhill through the woods, well marked with purple blazes. It passes two small waterfalls as the trail drops and follows creeks and crosses a little boardwalk along the way. Across the road Raven Cliff Falls travels for 2.2 miles (4.4 miles RT) to a viewing deck overlooking a beautiful gorge. The trail, heavily forested, has ups and downs and many tree roots, but arrives at a scenic overlook. Red blazes mark the way and at a trail intersection, at 1.4 miles, stay left to walk about 0.6 miles further to the observation deck. Part of the overlook is sheltered with benches to rest or eat lunch on and from the covered shelter or the viewing deck are beautiful views of the falls and across the Blue Ridge Mountains and Raven Cliff Mountain. Raven Cliff Falls, about one-forth mile away, is one of the highest falls in the state and is formed where Matthews Creek plunges 420 feet over high cliffs to drop, almost in layers, down the mountainside. The Dismal Trail, back at the intersection, will link into the Naturaland Trust Trail after 1.5 miles to take you closer to the falls but be advised this will be a long and taxing hike, over 8 miles roundtrip instead of just over four.

Caesars Head State Park is must-see park to visit for the dramatic views in all seasons. And in the fall the Hawk Watch program allows visitors to see hawks, eagles, ravens, falcons, kites and more migrating raptors swirling and soaring over the mountain ranges. For a side visit, not in the park, you might want to check the schedule for visiting the beautiful mountain top Frank W. Symmes

Chapel, or "Pretty Place" in the YMCA camp 6-7 miles past Caesars Head Park off Hwy 276. The chapel at the end of the camp road offers spectacular views across the Mountain Bridge Wilderness and is an inspiring spot for any to see.

A short distance from the Caesars Head Park entrance on SC Highway #11 is the Wildcat Wayside area managed by the park system and built by the CCCs in the 1930s for public enjoyment. You will see the Wildcat Wayside sign on the side of the road with a long pull-off parking area. You can see two waterfalls here. Lower Wildcat Branch Falls, 30 feet high, can be seen right off the highway. The 30-foot falls tumbles over a rocky embankment into a wide pool below. A trail to the side of the falls area, marked with yellow blazes and starting on stone steps, leads in a half-mile loop up into the woods and to another falls. At one forth mile the trail comes to Upper Wildcat Cascades falling over a granite wall before the trail winds back down again. Along the way are two other small cascades and an old chimney shelter built by the CCC with a historic marker.

21

Table Rock State Park

Upstate - Pickens County
Park Address: 158 Ellison Lane, Pickens, SC 29671
Park Size: 3,083 Acres   Month Visited: September
Directions: From the north via Hwy 25 or from the south via Hwy 276, turn on Hwy 11 (Geer Hwy) to the brown park sign; the park spreads on both sides of the highway, so first turn south to the visitor center.

Park Description:

Table Rock State Park sprawls across both sides of Highway #11. To begin an exploration of the park turn south at the East Gate Entrance on Ellison Road and drive to the park office and visitor center. The cabin-like building overlooks Lake Oolenoy, and the center has park information and maps plus a nice gift shop. Sixty-seven-acre Lake Oolenoy beside the visitor center is one of two lakes in Table Rock State Park. Carrick Creek feeds into Lake Oolenoy and then travels on across the road into Pinnacle Lake and beyond. Pretty Lake Oolenoy is especially popular for boating, kayaking, and fishing. The lake has two fine fishing piers, one handicap accessible, and a boat ramp.

Table Rock State Park, an early South Carolina park, was built in 1935 by the Civilian Conservation Corps (CCC) and many bridges, walls, and structures show the CCC's handiwork. The park has long been a favorite for campers with two campgrounds and a total of 94 sites. In addition, there are 16 cabins, 9 built by the CCC, and a beautiful CCC lodge on Pinnacle Lake, a popular spot for meetings, weddings, and other events. During the year the park hosts trail runs, educational programs, Fall Foliage Walks and regular Music on the Mountains bluegrass jams.

After stopping at the visitor center and checking out Lake Oolenoy, drive across Highway #11 into the larger section of the park to the north. Watch for a pull over on the left side of the road at the first overlook. Park and walk down the pathway to a bench and gorgeous view down the full length of Pinnacle Lake with Table Rock Mountain in the background. It's a pretty spot. The 1.9-miles Lake-

side Trail wanders along the lakeside here, winding its way over to the swim beach you can see in the far distance, and then circling the entire lake. Continuing up the main road leads to the Lodge, also worth a stop for the fine views from the deck behind it. The park road then winds uphill to a pull off on the right at the Table Rock Overlook where you can see stunning views of the 3,124-foot mountain. A marker at the overlook provides interesting historical information. It notes that Cherokee legend thought an enormous spirit once loomed over this mountain region. His shadow, spreading over the mountains with a bluish haze, gave the mountains their Blue Ridge name. The Cherokee also believed this giant spirit sat on lower Stool Mountain

and ate his meals off the higher and flatter Table Rock Mountain beside it. It's fun to imagine that as you stand at the overlook and look at these two tall mountain peaks.

Beyond the overlook the park road winds around to a side road to the White Oaks Campground, two park cabins, and the White Oaks picnic shelter. Continuing on leads to another side road winding down to the seasonal swim beach and boat rental area. This is a lovely spot with a broad sandy swimming beach, a raft with a high dive, the Hemlock Shelter on the hillside, and many picnic tables along the lakeside under shady trees. Across a wooden bridge is a nice children's playground and more picnic tables, and another access point to the Lakeside Trail which winds all the way around the lake. In season, visitors can rent canoes, kayaks, and paddle boats to enjoy on beautiful Pinnacle Lake. From points all along the trail and by the lake are views up to Table Mountain, making this area a lovely and memorable one.

Across the street from this recreation area is the park Nature Center. This is the point where most of the park trails originate and where hikers sign up to head out on the longer trails. Red blazed Table Rock Trail, 3.6 miles (7.2 mi RT) climbs up to the summit of Table Rock Mountain, offering stupendous views at the top and passing an old CCC trailside shelter along the way. Yellow-blazed Pinnacle Mountain Trail, 4.2 miles (8.4 mi RT) climbs up to Pinnacle Mountain and connects with the longer Foothills Trail traveling through South Carolina. A highlight on the Pinnacle Mountain Trail is a spur trail leading to Mill Creek Falls, a long 25-foot cascade spilling down the mountainside. Several other trails wind through the area, too, but the shortest and easiest to walk is the Carrick Creek Nature Trail. Like all the trails mentioned above, it begins right behind the Nature Center. We walked left on the Carrick Creek Trail loop to soon find two nice waterfalls. The first, at only about 100 yards up the trail, has a wooden platform, providing easy access to see and enjoy the falls. Not too much further up the trail is a stair-step cascade of small falls in the creek. Continuing on around the trail loop leads to more cascades and waterfalls in the creek and to views of Table Rock as the trail rises. Hiking the entire 2-miles trail loop, marked with green blazes, takes about an hour. This trail and the Lakeside Trail around Pinnacle Lake are the two easier walks in the park to enjoy.

After we explored a few of the trails out of the Nature Center, we followed the main road around the park to several side roads leading to park cabins and to more pavilions and picnic tables on the lake. Beyond the cabin area another side road leads to the second Table Rock camping area, an old store, recreation building and a large pavilion, known as Pinnacle Pavilion or The Barn. Not far from The Barn is another park trail, the Palmetto Trail. This trail is a rugged hiking and mountain bike trail covering a 12.3-miles section of the longer SC Palmetto Trail, marked with yellow blazes and running between the park and US Highway #178. Only a two-mile portion of the trail is inside the park boundary, with the next ten miles more difficult and remote.

After leaving the last campground section, follow the main road to the West Gate Entrance and back to Highway #11 again. You will want to put this beautiful state park on your "to visit" list.

Paris Mountain State Park

Upstate - Greenville County
Park Address: 2401 State Park Road, Greenville, SC 29609
Park Size: 1,540 Acres   Month Visited: September
Directions: From Hwy 276 (Poinsett Highway) above Greenville, take SC 253/E. Blue Ridge Drive north which becomes State Park Road, stay left at any intersections, continuing on State Park Road. Watch for the park sign and entrance on left, approximately 4 miles from the turn at Hwy 276.

Park Description:

Paris Mountain State Park was named for an early mountain settler, Richard Pearis, who was thought to be the first white man to settle in Greenville County in 1765. The Cherokee owned and hunted the lands then and Pearis married a Cherokee woman and established a store and mill. He attained large tracts of land from the Cherokee, including the mountain land that later in 1935 became the park. Paris Mountain State Park lies on a raised plateau and is the only mountain in the area making it a monadnock, which means an isolated mountain above a flat plain. The park has a long hatchet shape, its elevation rising from the lower handle to Piney Spur and Brissy Ridge in the larger, upper handle. The entry to the park is at the lower end of the hatchet and most of the park amenities lie there, also.

With Paris Mountain only about 5 miles north of downtown Greenville,

it is widely enjoyed by locals as well as visitors. The park offers swimming, picnicking, camping, hiking, and biking. It has one main lake, 13-acre Lake Placid, which is very accessible to the public. It also has two remote backcountry lakes accessible only by hiking trails—Mountain Lake and North Lake—and a fourth lake, Buckhorn Lake, inside Camp Buckhorn, which was once a camp for underprivileged chil-

dren. The former campground, with ten rustic cabins and a lodge, was built by the CCCs, and the old Buckhorn Lodge there is on the National Register of Historic Places. Many weddings, reunions, and meetings are held in this beautiful lodge on the lake but the camp area is gated and not open to the general public to tour.

As you enter the park and travel to the Visitor Center, you'll pass a pull-over stop at a picnic area leading to one of the park's pavilions and picnic tables by Lake Placid. A little further down the road at the visitor center, you can purchase a park map if you didn't bring one and enjoy the small museum and gift shop inside. From the broad back porch of the visitor center are scenic views down to Lake Placid and more picnic areas by the lake. A broad sandy beach leads out into the lake for swimming, with a swim raft a little ways from the shore. There are also two fishing docks, and in season, kayaks, canoes, and paddleboats can be rented. We found this area of the park busy even on a weekday afternoon.

Before leaving the visitor center area, don't miss walking to see the spill-way dam on the northeast end of Lake Placid. We followed the Lake Placid Trail to the dam starting just beyond the swim beach. It's an easy and pretty walk

moving through a picnic area with beautiful large trees before crossing a scenic wooden bridge over the creek. The trail then travels on through another picnic area and alongside the lake before swinging left to the dam and spillway. The pathway here drops steeply downhill to cross the stream below the dam on a wooden bridge before climbing a tier of rock steps to continue around the back-side of the lake. This is an easy-moderate loop hike less than a mile in length and an enjoyable one on a well-maintained pathway.

At the southwest end of Lake Placid, after returning from the spill-way, are access points to several other park trails. The park has 15 miles of hiking trails, rated from easy to difficult. By the bridge, the half-mile Turtle Trail, marked with red blazes, begins and wanders alongside the creek. This is a nice easy walk for families and the trail comes out across from the campground area. Also across the bridge at the end of the lake is an intersection of two more trails, the Lake Placid Trail and the 1.3-miles Mountain Creek Trail, a hiking and mountain bike trail. The Mountain Creek Trail also leads after a short walk to the park's outdoor amphitheatre where park programs, events and concerts are held, like the Folk Fest.

Across the road from the Visitor Center is the park's ball field and be-yond that recreation area, on a side road, is the park's large campground. This is a scenic campground with a smooth paved loop road and 39 paved sites. All have water and electric and some can accommodate RVs 35-40 feet. The campground area includes two large restrooms with hot showers and a dump station. The campground is also within walking or biking distance of the swim beach and lake area, nice for visitors.

About a mile on down the main road from the campground area are two

more pavilion and picnic areas. At the first, on the right, a connector trail leads to the ongoing Mountain Creek Trail. At the second on the left, Picnic Area #6, are two large pavilions along the creek with picnic tables and a big recreation field. The Sulphur Springs Trail begins directly across from the parking area. The entire loop hike is close to four miles in length, very rugged and strenuous in spots, but for a short, moderate 0.5-miles (1 mile RT) hike, you can walk in on the trail to the old dam and waterworks. This dam was built in 1890 to provide a reliable and safe water source for the city of Greenville. Gravity carried the water from the stream into town without the need for a pump. However, a valve house was built beside the dam to regulate the flow of the water from the reservoir. You can see the dam and the old valve house on this hike and a climb around the valve house leads to the water dammed above it.

The road beyond the Sulphur Springs area leads further into the park to the more remote hiking trails, most of which are both hiking and biking trails. These include the short but steep Fire Tower roadbed trail leading 0.4-mile uphill to the site where there used to be a fire tower and the 2.0-miles Kanuga Trail, also difficult. Nearby, the 2.4-miles Brissy Ridge Loop begins at the parking lot at the gate to Buckhorn Lodge. This yellow-blazed trail, also rated difficult, loops around Camp Buckhorn and is a strenuous, rocky and rooted trail. Brissy Ridge Trail and the Kanuga Trail both link to the backwoods one-mile Pipsissewa Trail. This trail rings around the perimeter of North Lake where there are

five backcountry campsites. Bikers and hikers love these trails, but note that all the park trails are closed to bikers on Saturdays.

Keowee-Toxaway State Park

Upstate - Pickens County
Park Address: 108 Residence Drive, Sunset, SC 29685
Park Size: 1,000 Acres   Month Visited: September
Directions: From the north via Hwy 25 or from the south via Hwy 276, turn and travel down SC Hwy 11 (Cherokee Foothills Scenic Highway) and watch for brown park signs; the park spreads on both sides of the highway, so first turn northwest to visitor center.

Park Description:

Keowee-Toxaway is a somewhat small state park but a gem for its beautiful lake views and hiking trails. The park lies in the foothills of the Blue Ridge Mountains along Lake Keowee in the midst of two state-managed wilderness areas, the Jocassee Gorges Management Area and the Keowee-Toxaway State Natural Area, making the area popular with hunters, anglers, boaters, and hikers. In the main area of the park is the Visitor Center, a campground, one rental cabin, a boat dock, and access points to hiking trails and backcountry campsites. Across the road is a loop road leading up to a picnic area and meeting facility, another hiking trail, and a side road leading to a group campground with cabins, pavilions, a meeting house and lake access.

The park Visitor Center, found on a side road to the right after entering the main park, looks like a pretty white church building. Inside are restrooms and a park office where you can pick up needed information. The office has maps, a gift shop, books, and some regional exhibits. However, note that the visitor center has limited hours, open in the mornings 11-12 am, closing, and then re-opening again from 4-5 pm.

Several hiking trails originate out of Keowee-Toxaway but the two most

popular ones begin directly behind the Visitor Center at a park
kiosk. Hikers can enjoy walking the short Natural Bridge
Trail Loop or extend their hike
into the longer Raven Rock
Trail. The Natural Bridge Nature Trail leads to a geological
natural wonder—a flat-topped
natural rock bridge that crosses
over Poe Creek. The trail to the
bridge is a moderate one, easy
to follow and blazed with white
diamonds along the way, first

moving through the woods in a gradual
descent. When the trail splits to make
its loop, stay to the right continuing on
downhill to the creek. There the trail
walks right out across the natural rock
bridge without you hardly realizing
you're crossing over Poe Creek at first.

After crossing, you can walk down to
the streamside to get a better look at
the bridge and the cave-like area un-
derneath it. Just beyond the bridge as
the trail curls watch for a short spur
path to a pretty waterfall and keep
your eye out for other cascades along
Poe Creek before the trail begins to
climb up the ridge back to its beginning. The uphill return hike is harder,
climbing up steep slopes and steps at
several points but you'll find a few rest
benches along the way. For most park
visitors this is a doable hike and takes
about one hour to walk.

To hike the longer Raven
Rock Loop Trail, 4.5-5 miles in length,
first follow the Natural Bridge Nature
Trail to the rock bridge over Poe Creek.
Shortly beyond the bridge, watch for a
trail intersection sign to turn onto the
Raven Rock Trail. This hike, beginning on a series of wooden steps, is
more strenuous than the nature loop

with many ups and downs. It's a narrow, single file trail with lots of rocks and roots, but it passes through a gorgeous mountain setting along its way and is a well-maintained trail. When the pathway comes to a "T" intersection and a second trail sign, follow to the right on the upper loop as the arrow points, which will lead to Raven Rock. The ongoing pathway winds in and out around the ridges and through boulder fields with huge rocks before eventually swinging left to walk along above Lake Keowee. There are many pretty vistas here across the lake where the trail hugs the ridgelines. A lovely stopping point for rest and lunch is down the spur path at Raven Rock the trail is named for, a big rock ledge above the lake. There are four backcountry campsites here for overnight camping and beautiful vistas across Lake Keowee. The return hike winds its way down the other side of the upper trail loop and then back to the parking area.

After returning to the Visitor's Center, drive on down the main road to the park's other areas. On a side road to the left on the shady hillside is a nice campground with 14 tent sites, a comfort station, and 10 lots for RVs. The 0.5-miles Lake Trail winds out of the back of the campsite to follow downhill to Lake Keowee. Leaving the campsite and continuing on the main road again leads to a large 3-bedroom cabin near the dock. At the small parking area at the dock are lovely views out over Lake Keowee and a nice boat ramp. This is a popular place

for kayakers and canoe enthusiasts to put their boats in the water. To the left of the parking lot by the boat ramp a row of steps leads down to a small beach spot and to the other end of the Lake Trail.

Across Highway #11 from the main section of Keowee-Toxaway park is a loop road leading to a nice picnic area and a big meeting room facility on the hillside. There are public restrooms at the meeting facility and the picnic tables are in sheltered covered buildings. We ate our lunch there and enjoyed this nice spot, exploring and also finding an old work road trail near the meeting room that we hiked a short distance on. To the north of this loop road is Crowe Creek Road, which leads back into the less developed area of the park and to the beginning of Poe Creek Trail not far from the highway. This is a long, but not difficult, 5.5-miles trail popular with hunters and anglers.

A newly opened section of the park is the new Camp Cedar Creek development on the southwest end of the park off Old Shallowford Bridge Road. The camp is gated to the general public but groups can rent the area for reunions, scout or church weekends, lakeside weddings, and other events. The area has 3 cabins, 10 tent campsites, 2 picnic shelters, a bathhouse and restroom facility, a fishing pier, and a lodge. The lodge building is large and very attractive with windows looking out on a beautiful piece of Lake Keowee. There is also a hiking trail in the camp area and a fire pit by the side of the lake.

Although small, Keowee-Toxaway has some interesting hiking trails, access to beautiful Lake Keowee, and fine views across the lake at many points. As an additional perk, the larger Table Rock and Devil's Fork state parks are not far away.

Devil's Fork State Park

Upstate - Oconee County
Park Address: 161 Holcombe Circle, Salem, SC 29676
Park Size: 622 Acres   Month Visited: September
Directions: From the north via Hwy 25 or from the south via Hwy 276, turn on Hwy 11 (Cherokee Foothills Scenic Hwy) and watch for brown park sign; turn left on Jocassee Lake Road and travel approximately 3 miles to camp entrance.

Park Description:

Devil's Fork State Park lies on the scenic 7,500-acre Lake Jocassee on the border of the Sumter National Forest in the midst of the Jocassee Gorges Wilderness area. Providing the only public access to the lake, the park is extremely popular with boating and fishing enthusiasts, and to all visitors who love the beautiful views out over the mountains and expansive lake. The lake's water is so clean and clear that it provides a wonderful premier location for all levels of scuba diving. The park even offers a remote walk-in ramp and diving platform, and an average of twenty to thirty feet visibility is common. Below the waters artifacts can be found, or have been placed, like an old fishing junk which divers love looking for. Nearby charter businesses provide dive charters and even scuba lessons for a fee.

Before exploring Devil's Fork stop at the park office, a long, attractive

building on a green hillside with lush landscaping and fine views out over the lake. At the office and visitor center you can pick up information, park maps, and there are restrooms and a gift shop. The park's Holcombe Meeting Room is also in the visitor center building complex, an excellent rental for small group events. Seasonally, the park rangers provide educational programs and hikes. One

of those programs is a spring educational hike on the 1.5-miles Oconee Bell Loop Trail. This nature trail can be found just behind the park office and leads in a 1.5-miles loop through the woods. It is one of only two sites where the rare spring blooming wildflower called the Oconee Bell can be found in the United States.

From the Visitor Center you can walk down to one the park's boat ramps and docks, where a long fishing pier extends far out into Lake Jocassee. There are three boat launch ramps here and the fishing pier offers a great spot for anglers or for walks out to view the lake. Canoe and kayak rentals are available at the visitor center for those wanting to get out on the lake and explore the large lake and its 90 miles of shoreline. At a kiosk by the water is a life jacket loaner station.

Swimmers and boaters can borrow and then return the life jackets provided by the park if they failed to bring their own.

Beside the boat dock across from the Visitor Center Hickory Hill Drive climbs to the park's 20 fully furnished rental villas, all modern with two or three bedrooms, fireplaces, and screened porches, many overlooking the lake. The villa area has its own boat dock area for those with boats or simply for visitors to enjoy for fishing or lake viewing, and the area has its own playground area for children. For non-campers these offer a fine place to stay for a vacation week on the lake.

For campers, the park has two campgrounds with 59 standard sites, some big enough for RVs up to 40 ft, two comfort stations with restrooms and hot showers, washers and dryers, and a dump station. There are also 25 nice walk-in tent sites with paved tent pads large enough for two tents, and many campsites are on the lake or near it. In addition there is a seasonal boat-in only campsite, with 13 spaces with tent pads but no facilities, two miles across the lake on a cove at Double Springs.

Near the campground area of the park is a side road, Buckeye Drive, that leads to a picturesque picnic area on the lake with two pavilions and a beautiful playground—a nice family spot to spend a day by Lake Jocassee. Swimming is allowed on the lake although no lifeguards are provided, and there is a concession area near the park picnic area. A second hiking trail, the 2.5-miles Bear Cove Trail, begins here—winding through the woods and campground and around a loop onto a peninsula with fine views of the lake. This trail was closed at the time we visited the park, so check with the park office to see if and when the trail will be reopened.

For a special lake outing, visitors can boat to several waterfalls accessible only by water. Lake Jocassee has four major falls and smaller falls to enjoy. There are even area guided waterfall boat tours, available near the park, and boats to rent to get to the falls. The major falls are Mill Creek Falls, where you can drive your boat right to the falls, Wrights Creek Falls you can walk behind, Laurel Fork Falls, a tall 80 ft falls at the end of a cove, and Whitewater Falls which can be seen, in part, at the extreme northwest corner of the lake. Whitewater Falls is said to be the highest series of falls east of the Mississippi with its sections spilling down the mountainside and covering over 1000 feet. Visitors can drive to see this latter falls if desired, by following north on SC 130 which becomes NC 281. The entrance to the falls in on the right just after crossing the NC state line, 6.9 miles and

about a 30 minute drive from the state park. Another short drive from the park is Twin Falls/Eastatoe Falls, a spectacular double-sided falls on Waterfalls Road off State Road 39-82. From the parking lot there is a short one fourth mile hike to the falls that takes about 15 minutes to walk. A pavilion has been built at the base of the falls where visitors can sit and enjoy the beauty of the spot before turning around to walk back.

For a week's vacation on a beautiful clear lake or only a weekend or day on the lake, this state park is a jewel—with its excellent campground, modern villas, fishing piers, boat docks, and lovely spots for family picnics.

Oconee Station State Historic Park

Upstate - Oconee County
Park Address: 500 Oconee Station Road, Walhalla, SC 29691
Park Size: 210 Acres   Month Visited: September
Directions: From the north via Hwy 25 or from the south via Hwy 276, turn and travel down SC Hwy 11 (Cherokee Foothill Scenic Highway). Watch for a park directional sign and turn on Oconee Station Road; follow to right turn into park at park sign.

Park Description:

Oconee Station is one of South Carolina's historic parks. Although small, it has a number of interesting sites to see and some memorable trails to explore. The park road comes to an end at a parking area near two park structures, a small office and restrooms. Beside the office, that has limited hours, is a pretty shaded picnic area. Winding around behind the picnic area by a log fence is a roadbed that leads to one of the park's hiking trails, which is also a Connector Trail to Oconee State Park. By road the distance between the parks is 16.2 miles, but although the Connector is a shorter route between the parks, even most veteran hikers don't advise it as an easy access route from park to park. The Connector Trail begins walking through the woods and then across the creek on a wooden footbridge but then rises steadily in an upward march to Station Mountain. It's a strenuous, challenging hike with lots of switchbacks, spur trails and intersections, not all clearly marked, but the views are stunning.

What Oconee Station State Historic Park is most famous for are its two historic sites, the Oconee Station Blockhouse and William Richards House. In the 1700s before either structure was built, the entire Oconee region belonged to the Cherokee. As white settlers moved into the area and Indian attacks grew severe, the British sent Lt. Colonel Archibald Montgomerie, the 11th Earl of Eglinton, in 1757 with soldiers from England to the American Colonies to build blockhouses for the settlers' protection. The Oconee Station blockhouse was erected before 1760 to provide protection and this structure is n o w the only remaining blockhouse structure built in this early Colonial Period and is on the National Register of Historic Places.

Three Richards brothers traveled with Montgomerie from England and decided to stay in the area. Stories say they stayed and kept the blockhouse until the Revolution when troops were removed. It was William Richards who later built the brick home beside the blockhouse in 1805, thought to be the first brick house ever built in the northeast corner of South Carolina and also now on the National Register of Historic Places. Richards owned thousands of acres of land and was a prosperous merchant and land owner, and he was buried in the area after his death.

At a signpost across from the main parking lot, follow the short pathway up to see both historic structures. Near the stone blockhouse structure, a plaque explains when the blockhouse was constructed in 1792 and when decommissioned. Some Revolutionary fighting took place in the Oconee Station area but after the war the property became privately owned and served as a family home and farm into the twen-

tieth century. After the Revolutionary War, William Richards established a trading post in the old blockhouse, used by settlers and the Cherokee, and in 1805 he built his brick home next door, which is surprisingly well preserved. In the early 19th century the station also served as a stage coach stop. In 1976 the entire site was purchased for the park from Edward Fearney. Tours of the historic structures can be scheduled on Saturdays and Sundays in the afternoon.

After visiting both historic structures and touring the grounds around them, visitors can walk the 1.5-miles Nature Trail loop that leads into the forest and then curls around a large pond. The trail begins at a sign on the road just past the parking lot. A kiosk there shows a park map and how the Oconee Station Trail will curl around the pond and then over the dam and back to the beginning. Swing to the left as the loop intersects. The trail is somewhat narrow with roots and rocks but scenic. Fern and mushroom and a wide variety of trees are seen along the way and glimpses of the pond to the right now and then. In spring wildflowers abound in this area. Just before the half way point of the trail, a path to the left says "Falls" and points to another trail. But continue on to the right to stay on the Nature Trail loop. It soon turns and winds around the backside of the pond or lake, climbing slightly up and down before swinging around to cross the creek back to the trail's beginning. This trail is an easy family walk.

Taking the turning to the falls at the Nature Trail intersection leads uphill to Oconee Station Road and over to meet the Station Cove Falls Trail. An easier way to hike to the falls is to drive back up the Oconee Station Road from the parking lot, watching for a kiosk on the side of the road in less that a quarter mile. There is room for about six cars to park here. From this point the easy pathway winds in a well-maintained moderate walk for 1.6-miles to the falls. This trail, too, is an easy family hike, winding through the woods with only moderate ups and downs. Another intersecting trail part way along the route connects to the ongoing Connector Trail leading to Oconee State Park. As the Station Cove Falls Trail moves on through the woods it passes over a short wooden bridge over Station Creek before arriving at the base of Station Cove Falls. This is a beautiful 60-foot waterfall that tumbles and cascades over a broad rock bluff into a pool below. Large boulders around the base of the falls provide a nice place to rest or picnic before turning to make the hike back to your car. This in and out hike is 3.2 miles round trip and makes a nice ending trip to a visit to this interesting park.

To learn more about the history of this area, plan a visit to the Oconee History Museum at 123 Brown's Square Drive in nearby Walhalla. Exhibits feature many artifacts from the past from early settlers and Native Americans. Nearby at 70 Short Street is The Museum of the Cherokee in South Carolina, open Thursday, Friday, and Saturday from 11-4 and containing many Indian exhibits remembering the rich heritage of Native Americans.

Oconee State Park

Upstate - Oconee County
Park Address: 624 State Park Road, Mountain Rest, SC 29644
Park Size: 1,165 Acres   Month Visited: September
Directions: From the north via Hwy 25 or from the south via Hwy 276, turn and travel down Hwy 11 (Cherokee Foothills Scenic Highway). Turn on Hwy 28 through Walhalla and turn right on Hwy 107 just after Mountain Rest Cafe; follow Hwy 107 to park sign on right and into the Park.

Park Description:

Oconee State Park was one of the early South Carolina parks built by the Civilian Conservation Corps (CCC). It's a rustic, scenic park with Oconee Lake in its center. The park offers camping and tent sites, picnic areas and shelters, a swim beach, canoe and kayak rentals, a miniature golf course, hiking trails, and park cabins built by the CCC. In front of the green-roofed visitor center is a CCC worker statue and inside the center is the park office and visitor center, a gift shop, and a Meeting Room that can accommodate up to 50 people. The park has a second meeting center for larger groups that also has a stage. Behind and to the sides of the visitor center are picnic areas, a pavilion, barn, and a large children's playground including a popular 18-hole mini-carpet golf course.

Across from the miniature golf area is a trading post and the entrance to the park campground area. All the camping sites have water and electric and there are several restroom areas, a dump station, and a second children's play-

ground. The park also offers 15 tent sites and a primitive group camping area that can be reserved. Several of the campsites look out over the smaller 12-acres Campground Lake, a nice place for fishing with a small fishing pier on the lake. The Oconee Trail starts near the beginning of the campground by the outdoor amphitheater and circles for 2.3 miles behind Campground Lake to travel into the woods. At 1.6 miles the trail

intersects the Old Waterwheel Trail and then continues on to its end at the Foothills Trail head. The hike is 4.6 miles from beginning to end and takes about 2-3 hours to walk.

Beyond the road to the campground is another nice trail to walk. Park by the miniature golf area and walk a short distance to a sign on the left of the road saying "Waterwheel" and then follow the trail to a waterwheel by the dam at the end of Oconee Lake. The original waterwheel powered a pump to provide drinking water for Oconee Park until the 1940s. Although this replica isn't the original waterwheel, many pieces of the original were brought here and the wheel recreated, making it an interesting spot to visit. An informative plaque explains the wheel's history and a side trail wanders up to the spillway dam. You can see the remnants of the old original waterwheel, if desired, on the Old Waterwheel Trail, which begins at the Foothills Trail head or behind the cabin area not far from it.

A side trail that winds around the waterwheel leads to the park's recre-

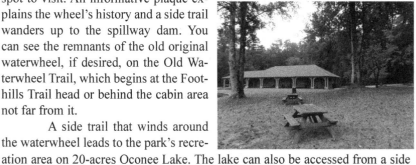

ation area on 20-acres Oconee Lake. The lake can also be accessed from a side road behind the park office where there is a parking area but we enjoyed walking

in to the lake from the waterwheel. At this south end of Oconee Lake is a beautiful green picnic area, swim beach, and boat rental shed where canoes, jon boats, and kayaks can be rented. Beside the beach and boat rental area is a long rustic bathhouse, built by the CCC, with a broad, shady front porch that used to be a Tea Room in the past. By the lake is a sandy beach and out in the lake is a swim raft with a high dive. This entire area by the lake is lovely and also provides another access point to the 1.2-miles Lake Trail circling Lake Oconee.

Continuing on main road past the trail to the waterwheel leads to two of the park cabin areas. Oconee park has five one-bedroom cabins and thirteen two-bedroom cabins in three sections in the park. Many of the park cabins look right out onto the lake from pretty screened porches.

Near the cabin roads you will also find the trailhead and parking area for the Foothills Trail. The long Foothills Trail, a National Recreation Trail, spans 77 miles from Oconee State Park to Table Rock State Park and is maintained by the Foothills Trail Conference. Several extensive multi-day hikes can be planned from this point but visitors can enjoy other shorter hikes beginning here, too. At the end of the Foothills Access Trail the path splits at a sign and hikers can follow to the right all the way to Tamassee Knob. This 8.2-miles RT hike is a rugged, strenuous one that climbs some steep cliffs but leads at its end to a knob with breath taking views. For a shorter more doable walk, hike only to the fine vistas on nearby Oconee Mountain and then turn around and return. The second route from the trail intersection split leads left along the Foothills Trail to Hidden Falls Trail. The first mile and a half of this walk is relatively flat before turning right on a spur trail to the falls, where the path grows steeper. Watch for a small cascade on the right of the spur called Disappearing Falls that drops underground. After a little more walking, the trail ends at the falls, which tumbles over granite ledges to

drop 60 feet—if the weather hasn't been too dry. The entire hike from the parking lot to the falls is appx 2.75 miles or 5.50 miles roundtrip.

After exploring this area of the park, return back to the visitor center and follow the road to the right to reach Oconee State Park's other sections. This road first curls down to the lake on a side road and then travels back through the woodlands to a left turn to the Barracks lodge area. The Barracks is a group facility for up to sixteen, with bathrooms, a kitchen, an outdoor picnic area and a fire ring in a quiet part of the park.

Continuing on the main road past the Barracks leads to a pullover parking spot and access to two other park trails. The Wormy Chestnut Trail crosses the road here to continue its loop route up into the woods, around and back again. This is one of the park's easier trails, beginning off the Lake Trail, but you can walk only this upper loop section by itself if you wish. Keep your eye open for some CCC structures along this trail and a stone dam crossing. You will also find links to the Palmetto Trail here. The park road beyond this trail area leads to a third cabin road on the north side of the lake and the end of the park. Return from this point down the road you traveled on back to the park entrance.

Oconee State Park was a great park to visit. The park offers a number of educational and special events throughout the year and hosts square dancing and bluegrass music during the summer months. Restaurants, shopping, and other venues can be found in nearby Walhalla in this upstate region rich with beauty, history, and a multitude of interesting tourist attractions.

Lake Greenwood State Park

Upstate - Greenwood County
Park Address: 302 State Park Road, Ninety Six, SC 29666
Park Size: 914 Acres   Month Visited: October
Directions: From Interstate 26, turn southeast on Hwy 72 at Clinton; follow Hwy 72 through Mountville; becomes 72/221 after crossing the Saluda River bridge; at Coronaca turn left on Hwy 246; stay left for about five miles to intersection of 246 and 702; stay left on Hwy 702 and follow appx 7 miles to park on left.

Park Description:

Lake Greenwood State Park lies out in the rural countryside about twenty-five minutes from Greenwood, South Carolina, on 11,400-acre Lake Greenwood. The lake was formed by the hydroelectric dam, built across the Saluda River in 1940, to generate power for the Greenwood area. The new lake with its 212 acres of beautiful shoreline soon became a favorite spot for boating, fishing, and lake recreation. Lake Greenwood State Park, opened in 1938, was one of the early parks built in South Carolina by the CCC and many of its original structures still stand. The park has 125 campsites, 4 picnic shelters, 2 boat ramps and a long fishing pier, plus bike and walking trails.

The perfect place to start your visit at this park is to drive down the loop road to the park office and visitor center. This long rustic building has a

large meeting room and a beautiful patio across the back of the building with views across Lake Greenwood. It's a gorgeous site for events, and paved walkways from the center lead down to scenic spots along the lake, fishing piers, old rock walls, and a boathouse. Inside the visitor center, besides the office and meeting room, is the historic Drummond Center Museum. This interesting exhibit offers

an account of the history of the parks and the Civilian Conservations Corps and New Deal work teams. The museum is named for state senator John Drummond, who served for 42 years in the state legislature and was also a World War II pilot and paratrooper. Drummond, awarded the Distinguished Flying Cross, two Purple Hearts, three Battle Stars, nine Air Medals, and a Presidential Citation, was a great patriot and 'man of the people.'

Moving on to explore other areas of the park, we soon found lush green picnic areas and pavilions on the lake and a long fishing pier. Other side roads led into the park's campgrounds, most tucked onto fingers in the lake with fine lakeside views and restrooms with hot showers. Most sites were full service sites for RVs or tent camping with water and electric hookup and a dump station. The waterfront sites in the park's campground areas make for great boat access and fishing for campers. Visitors can put their own boats in at the park's boat ramps, and fish off the piers or banks. Rods and reels are available for loan at the park office, too, through the Tackle Loaner Program sponsored by the South Carolina De-

partment of Natural Resources. Fish caught on Lake Greenwood include perch, bream, stripers, crappie, and bass. The park also has a primitive camping area for organized groups like scouts, off a side road beyond the main park road, with its own boat ramp, fire pit, restrooms, picnic tables and a covered shelter.

The park has a nice 0.8-miles nature trail that begins at the recreation building at the beginning of Campground #1. This loop trail is easy to follow with blue blazes marking the way. There is also a longer 4.21-miles Scenic Shoreline Trail winding along the banks of the lake, crossing over several bridges. The trail offers a look at herons and turtles on the lake, many bird species, and passes several good spots for fishing. Another trail, the Forest Trail, winds through the woods and is used by both hikers and bikers.

The park allows swimming in most sections of the lake although there isn't a designated swim beach area. Lake Greenwood offers various programs and events during the year and in the spring there are many wildflowers to see, including lush purple wisteria in early April. Each June, the park is the host site for the South Carolina Festival of Flowers Triathlon, a swim, bike, and run event.

History Note:

The Great Depression in the United States (1929-1941) began with the Wall Street Stock Market Crash of 1929 and began years of bank crashes, unemployment, plunging incomes, and widespread poverty and despair for Americans. It has been called the worst economic downturn in the history of the industrialized world. A bright spot in this dark period was Franklin D. Roosevelt's creation of the Civilian Conservation Corps (CCC) in 1933. This work relief program provided jobs to young men from 1933 to 1942 when World War II ended the program.

The men of the CCC planted over three billion trees, engaged in environmental enrichment programs stopping erosion, designed and created roads, and helped to build state parks all over the United States. In South Carolina the men of the CCC built sixteen state parks. The Civilian Conservation Corps Museum, part of the John Drummond and Holly Self Drummond Environmental Conference Center, at Lake Greenwood State Park is one of the few museums in the United States dedicated solely to the men of who built more than 700 new state parks.

The museum at Lake Greenwood State Park has interactive exhibits that colorfully describe the work, life, and times of the CCC's projects in South Carolina. It also tells about how the lake was built, about the WPA program in South Carolina, and depicts the history of the South Carolina parks. Take time when visiting this park to go through this interesting museum documenting the legacy of the CCC.

Ninety Six National Historic Site

Upstate - Greenwood County
Park Address: 1103 SC Hwy 248, Ninety Six, SC 29666
Park Size: 1,022 acres   Month Visited: October
Directions: From Interstate 26, take Exit #74. Travel appx. 30 miles on Hwy 34 through Newberry and Chappels into the town of Ninety Six. Then take Hwy 248 for two miles to park.

Park Description:

The United States was involved in the Revolutionary War with the British from April 9, 1775, to September 3, 1783. A battle called "The Seige of Ninety Six" occurred late in the war years. The British, successful in taking Charleston, had moved inland to win much of South Carolina. However, by mid May of 1781, the only significant British garrison remaining in the state, besides Charleston, was at Ninety Six, a post occupied by 550 experienced Loyalists under the command of Lt Col John Cruger. Colonists in this area held mixed loyalties and many retained their allegiance to the British for their protection from the Cherokee and for land grants received.

On May 22nd, 1781, Continental Army Major General Nathanael Greene led 1000 troops against the British at Ninety Six in a nearly month-long siege. At the end of the siege attacks, with heavy reinforcements of 2000 British soldiers only 30 miles away, Greene was forced to call off the attack and retreat into North Carolina. The war ended two years later at the Seige of Yorktown in Virginia. When the Loyalists withdrew from Ninety Six they burned the town behind them.

The town of Ninety Six, at the time of the Revolutionary War, was a major crossroads in western South Carolina. Cherokee legends say the town, and other towns and creeks with similar numeric names like Six Mile and Twenty One, were named by a Cherokee maiden, Isaqueena, to try to alert her British sweetheart of upcoming Indian attacks. Other stories say traders created the town names to note the distances from the Cherokee village of Keowee to SC towns. Not until the 1960s was the Ninety Six battle site listed on the National Register and declared a Historic Landmark in 1973. Shortly afterward in 1976, the 1,022-acre Ninety Six property was established as a National Historic Site and is maintained by the National Park Service. Except

for a few remaining natural features in the park, most sites and structures in the park are replicas to an important period in American history and to the longest siege of the Revolutionary War.

Knowing the background of the park is helpful before exploring it. However at the park visitor center is a small museum with artifacts and history information. In addition, free brochures are available at the center and visitors can rent a self-guided tour of the park or buy a video about the Ninety Six battle. Also a fine movie *Ninety Six: Crossroads of a Revolution* can be viewed by request in the visitor center theater.

Just beyond the center, the paved one-mile interpretive trail begins, winding its way through the park in a scenic loop. A Walking Tour write-up of the park, found inside the free park brochure, details each point along the route, explaining historic spots, roads, reconstructed battle sites, the stockade, and other buildings. Early along the trail and at a later point, too, the trail crosses Spring Branch, the stream which provided the water source for the village of Ninety Six and the Loyalists. Along the route at many points are colorful signposts explaining the places visitors are viewing along the pathway. The trail passes Loyalist fortifications—stockades, ditches, trenches, and other earthworks, a rifle tower, old mine, and cannons—all created to depict the original structures of the British garrison. Also along the

51

walking trail are black metal statuary of soldiers and settlers to help bring scenes to life.

Midway around the trail is the Star Fort. This fort was the heart of the British defense at Ninety Six, an unusual 8-pointed fortified structure, not easy to construct, but it created a great defense point from which soldiers could fire from many different positions. Erosion has diminished the original walls, once 14-feet high and 10-15-feet thick, but the Star Fort is one of the few original structures in the park.

The pathway continues winding past the fort to the site of the Town of Ninety Six which once had 12 dwellings, a courthouse, jail, blacksmith, and other structures in the 1700s village. A nice kiosk shows pictures of what the village might have looked like. Beyond the village area is the Stockade Fort built to guard the town's water supply and James Holmes' house. Past the fort the walking trail ends at a picnic area near the Logan Log House, built by an early settler Andrew Logan and dating from the 1700s. The house, with an outdoor cooking oven, is furnished like a tavern today and called the Black Swan Tavern. Many of the park's programs and events are held here. On the park grounds are also a small 27-acres lake with a nature trail, a recreation area, fishing pier and boat launch.

History Note:

The town of Ninety Six became a major military site in the Revolutionary War in part because so many important roads passed through the town. Three historic roads intersected at the old Ninety Six town site and markers note these

roads within the park. The Charleston Road was the major trade route from Ninety Six to Charleston, SC, which was called Charles Town then. It was also called the Gouedy Trail since earlier it led to Robert Gouedy's trading post. The Whitehall Road, traveling north from Augusta, Georgia, led to Brigadeer General Andrew Williamson's plantation home, called White Hall, near Ninety Six. In the 1700s many roads led to White Hall as William was a very wealthy man and the leader of the American Militia at Ninety Six before the British took it in 1775. Island Ford Road, now a sunken roadbed from all the travelers that passed over it, led north and was the road that American Troops, led by Col Greene, traveled across to hopefully take the British fort at Ninety Six.

Hamilton Branch State Park

Upstate - McCormick County
Park Address: 111 Campground Road, Plum Branch, SC 29845
Park Size: 731 acres   Month Visited: October
Directions: From I-26 take exit #74 onto Hwy 34. Follow through
Newberry and Ninety Six, then left on 178/221. Continue on 221
through McCormick to Plum Branch south to park on right.

Park Description:

     Hamilton Branch State Park was one of several SC parks we visited set
on the J. Strom Thurmond Lake. This huge 71,100-acres lake was created by the
construction of the J. Strom Thurmond Dam. The dam, begun in the 1940s, met
with several delays but was completed in 1954. A drive to the dam from Hamilton Branch, only 13 miles away, would create an interesting side trip. The giant
dam is 1,096 feet across and 204 feet high, with enough concrete in the dam to
build a sidewalk from South Carolina to California! Also at the dam's visitor
center is a museum depicting the history of the dam, plus a nice park below the
dam with a swim beach and recreation area.

     Hamilton Branch State Park, the closest SC state park to the dam, sits
on a pretty peninsula jutting out into the J. Strom Thurmond Lake. The park offers two boat ramps for access to the lake, campsites, picnic areas, and hiking

and biking trails. The visitor center near the park entrance can provide information and a park map and offers a nice picnic area beside it with umbrella-covered tables. Near the center are the trailheads for the park's two hiking trails. One is the short and easy 0.3-miles Hamilton Branch Connector which leads across the highway to the longer 7.1-miles Stevens Creek Trail for both

hiking and biking. The park's Paleo Hiking Trail, a short 1.5-miles woods walk, also starts by the visitor center at a fenced entrance. This is an easy trail to follow with white signs and black arrows along its way.

Heading down the pretty wooded road beyond the visitor center leads back into the park and to picnic pavilions and campgrounds. The park has several pleasant campground areas with 173 standard sites with water and electricity and 11 tent sites with water only. Some sites can accommodate large RVs and many sit right on the shores of the lake. The park has eight comfort stations with hot showers and two dump stations making this a really delightful park for campers. There is also a primitive group camping area for organized groups, with its own private restrooms, picnic tables, and a fire ring, that can accommodate even large groups up to 400.

Hamilton Branch offers fishing, swimming, boating and other lake recreational opportunities and the park also provides bicycle rentals at the visitor center. In addition, guests can check out recreational equipment at the center for soccer, kickball, horseshoes, and Frisbee fun. Even playing cards, games, and puzzles are available for loan.

Beautiful views out across J. Strom Thurmond Lake can be found down every park side road and all these lovely areas in this park are easy to access. Near the beginning of the park a long side road leads to the park's day access area, with two large pavilions, picnic areas, a big children's playground, and a boat dock with a small boat ramp beside it.

Baker Creek State Park

Upstate - McCormick County
Park Address: 863 Baker Creek Rd, McCormick, SC 29835
Park Size: 1,305 acres   Month Visited: October
Directions: From I-26, take exit #74 onto Hwy 34. Follow through
Newberry and Ninety Six, then left on 178/221. Continue on 221
to McCormick, then on 378 south to park on right.

Park Description:

     Baker Creek State Park is a seasonal park, open from March 1st through
either September 30th or October 31st, so be sure to check with the park's website
to be sure this park is open before visiting. The park borders a finger of the J.
Strom Thurmond Lake with access to the main channel. A relatively new state
park that opened in 1967, Baker Creek sits on land leased from the U.S. Army
Corps of Engineers.The park offers waterfront campsites, lake activities and hiking and biking trails.

     The main visitor center at Baker Creek is not located near the entrance
of the park but at the end of the main park road in a beautiful pavilion overlooking the lake. At the pavilion is the park office and a large, covered open-air meeting facility ideal for group gatherings, meetings, weddings, and other events.
The view across the lake from the back of the pavilion is stunning and on the

grounds around the pavilion are a horseshoe pit, volleyball and basketball courts, as well as paths along the lake and picnic tables. Not far from the pavilion is the beginning of the park's ten-mile mountain biking and hiking trail. A sign with an arrow points the way from the main road to the trailhead with a registration mailbox and arrows mark the route as it circuits through the park.

Off a side road not far from the park office are the park's two campground areas. There are 50 standard sites with water and electric, a dump station and a comfort station with restrooms and hot showers. The campsites are pretty with picnic tables and many campsites sit right by the lake. The 0.8-miles Wild Mint Nature Trail winds in a loop route out of Campground #2 following green posts with white letters. It's mostly an easy walking trail winding through the woods with lake overlooks and a footbridge.

On the park's other side road is a boat ramp and another scenic picnic area on the water. The park's second Walking Trail, 0.7 miles in length, begins near the boat ramp to loop around through the woods and then near the lake before winding its way back to the parking lot again.

Although Baker Creek park is somewhat small it has nice facilities and campgrounds with gorgeous lake views throughout the park. It's a fishing, boating, and lake paradise located in a quiet rural area, and it's easy to see why the park is a popular spot for visitors and locals during the warm months when it is open.

Hickory Knob State Park

Upstate - McCormick County
Park Address: 1591 Resort Drive, McCormick, SC 29835
Park Size: 1,091 acres   Month Visited: October
Directions: From I-26, take exit #74 onto Hwy 34. Follow through Newberry and Ninety Six, then left on 178/221. Continue on 221 to McCormick, then take Hwy 378W to SC Hwy 7. Turn on Resort Road at park sign into the park.

Park Description:

Hickory Knob State Park is the only full service resort in South Carolina's state park system. It sits on the shorelines along 71,000-acres Strom Thurmond Reservoir on the Savannah River. The park offers golf, hiking and mountain biking, skeet shooting, archery, fishing, and boating. It has a lodge, restaurant, store, motel and cabin accommodations, a convention center, campground, tennis courts, playgrounds, pavilions and picnic areas.

The best way to begin an exploration of this park is to follow Resort Drive, the main park road, to its end at the park office, visitor center and lodge. Inside the center is a park store, a fine meeting room, the reservation desk for the lodge, and a large restaurant. Visitors can stay in the lodge or in the nearby cabin-villas and motel rooms, most overlooking the lake. In addition, the Barrack facility, with four bedrooms, is great for groups. A pool is available for lodge and cabin guests and the park also has a horseshoe pit, a nice children's playground, volleyball and basketball courts, and other outdoor games, along with a putting green, outdoor picnic areas by the center and on the lake, an amphitheatre, a dock and fishing pier. We enjoyed chatting with a big group of friends who were picnicking by the visitor center.

The Hickory Knob Restaurant provides buffet-style meals, or off the menu choices, for breakfast, lunch, and dinner and the spacious dining room can seat up to 150 guests. In addition to the restaurant for group gatherings, the resort has several meeting facilities—the Mt. Carmel and McCormick meeting rooms for smaller groups and the lovely Convention Center building, across the street from the visitor center, for larger groups up to 100. This building has its own kitchen, restrooms, fireplace and an outdoor area overlooking the lake. All these park amenities are clustered conveniently within walking distance of each other on the end of the Resort Road loop.

Returning up the main road leads to other scenic points in the park. The historic French Guillebeau House sits on a shady property under the trees. The house was built in the 1700s in the Huguenot Settlement of New Bordeaux. The Huguenots, who fled to America in search of religious freedom, built seven colonies in South Carolina and there are still remnants of the settlement and township they built in nearby McCormick. The Guillebeau cabin, originally owned by New Bordeaux resident Andre Guillebeau, was relocated to the park in 1983 and visitors to the park can stay overnight in the home by reservation. Across the street from the cabin, a side road winds

down to the park's boat ramp. Canoes, kayaks, and paddleboards are available for rent here and boats can access the lake from the boat ramp or tie up at the dock overnight. This is a good spot for fishing in the cove, or off the pier, and fishing rods and reels are available for loan at the Hickory Knob park office.

Driving on along Resort Drive leads by the resort's golf course and to the clubhouse. The 18-hole Hickory Knob Golf Course was designed by Tom Jackson and offers a challenging assortment of fairway widths, slopes and contours, many alongside the lake. By the clubhouse is a practice green and driving range and the clubhouse has a full-service pro shop, an outdoor deck with seating looking out over the golf course and lake, and The Shagbark Snack Bar offering meals and beverages.

On the other side of the road from the golf course is a skeet range and an archery course. The beginning of the Beaver Run hiking and mountain bike trail begins here, too, winding along on a dirt path through the woods for 2.5 miles.

Past the golf course the Campfire Road leads to the park's campground with 44 campsites with water and electric. The campground has restrooms with hot showers and a dump station, and although small, the campground is scenic and most sites are near or on the lake.

A short distance from the campground road, near the park entrance on the hill, is a red barn, called the Long Cane Center, ideal for large group meetings or events. Beside the barn and across the street from it are

the park's two other hiking trails. The
Lakeview Loop Trail for hiking and
biking travels for 7.2 miles on a challenging course along the ridges above
the lake and back. Across the street
is the beginning of the Turkey Ridge
Loop, a shorter 2.5-miles hiking and
biking woods loop trail. All three
park bike trails are favorites with bike
enthusiasts, with their rollercoaster
pathways and beautiful water views at
nearly every turn.

Of all the state parks in South
Carolina, this one offers the most diversity of things to do and see. The
golf course, lodge, and the beauty of
the lake make this park an especially
memorable one.

For more explorations
around the area, nearby McCormick
County, first settled in the 1700s, is
steeped in history, and visitors can
travel to a number of interesting spots
in McCormick only eleven miles
away. Just outside McCormick, the
Heritage Gold Mine Park can be visited during open days and hours. Visitors can pan for gold, see the museum,
and learn about the 1850s mine. Gold
prospered this region and an old street
in McCormick is still actually called
Gold Street.

In downtown McCormick
are many old buildings listed on the
National Register of Historic Places.
The J.J. Dorn House on Gold Street,
was the home of SC Senator Joseph
Jennings Dorn and houses a museum.
Nearby is the historic train depot,
dating back to 1911, the McCormick
Country Courthouse, constructed in
1923, and the Colonial Revival Style
Hotel Ketura built in 1910, all on the
National Register.

Calhoun Falls State Park

Upstate - Abbeville County
Park Address: 46 Maintenance Shop Rd, Calhoun Falls, SC 29628
Park Size: 318 acres   Month Visited: October
Directions: From I-26 take Clinton exit onto Hwy 72. Follow Hwy 72 to Greenwood and through Abbeville to Calhoun Falls, then north on Hwy 81 to Calhoun Falls State Park Road and park sign.

Park Description:

Calhoun Falls State Park was not named after a waterfall, as we expected, but after the nearby town, Calhoun Falls. The town and park are both named for James Edward Calhoun (1798-1889) brother-in-law of statesman and Vice President John C. Calhoun. James served as a lieutenant in the U.S. Navy and built Millwood Plantation approximately five miles from the town of Calhoun Falls on the Savannah River. Millwood was a thriving 10,000-acre plantation with a gristmill, two ferries and a cotton gin that James Calhoun operated successfully for his entire life. Remnants of the plantation still exist and Millwood Plantation was one of the largest plantations in South Carolina. The plantation's gristmill and millrace at Trotter's Shoals had a 14-foot waterfall to power its turbines, very unusual for its time, which is probably where the name Calhoun Falls came from.

The building of the Richard B. Russell Dam and Lake by the U.S. Army Corps of Engineers in 1983-1984 brought change to the entire area and led to the creation of the Calhoun Falls State Park, only three miles from the dam. Lake Russell is one of the less-developed reservoirs in South Carolina with wonderful fishing for bream, crappie, bass, walleye, stripers, and catfish.

The park has boating, fishing, hiking, biking, swimming, and camping. It offers playgrounds, boat ramps, picnic shelters, tennis and basketball courts, and a park store. The park also manages the nearby 6,239-acre McCalla State Natural Area, with a ten-mile equestrian trail and more fishing opportunities.

On entering the Calhoun Falls State Park drive down the main road through the woods and follow the signs to the visitor center on a peninsula jutting out into 26,650-acre Lake Russell. Because this park is newer, the roads and facilities are especially nice and the campground areas have large, shady, level sites. At the visitor center and office, in addition to park information, a store and gift shop offer limited grocery items, snacks, tackle supplies,

bait and loaner rods and reels, and firewood. One of the two hiking trails, the Mariner Nature Trail, winds out from the parking lot of the visitor center, along the lake and over to the Primitive Camping Area.

Close to the park office is a boat ramp and a beautiful marina with 36 rental boat slips. The marina provides water, electricity, hot showers, a refueling station, and access to sewage pump-out. This is really a gorgeous, memorable spot in the park. Fishing is good on Lake Russell and anglers catch warm and cold water species like bass, crappie, perch, spotted bass, warmouth, bluegill, sunfish, stripers, catfish, and a few trout. The natural shoreline offers great spots to fish in the brush and near rocks that many fish like to use as cover. Several bass tournaments are held on Lake Russell.

Heading back up the main road we explored the park's first campground area with beautiful camping spots on the water, nice playgrounds, an amphitheater, restrooms and great streets to bike and walk on. The park has two campground areas, each with restrooms and showers, and a dump station, and there is a washer/dryer available in one of the campground areas. The Green Light fishing pier stretches far out into Lake Russell off a small side road and it is not hard to see why so many people love to come camping in this state park. We even saw wild deer and turkey.

Further up the main road another road winds down to two day use areas for the public with tennis and basketball courts, picnic areas and two large shelters. Shelter #2 has areas for changing to enjoy the pretty sand swim beach built along the lakefront. It's easy to imagine families enjoying a day at this nice spot. A short walk or drive away is the other day use area with another

shelter and picnic tables along the lake, a second playground and the basketball court. All areas have good access to the lake and the little coves on Lake Russell around the park are great spots for canoes and kayaks.

The park's second hiking trail, the 1.7-miles Cedar Bluff Nature Trail, begins at the day use area, following blue blazes through a woods loop and over several footbridges near the lake. The trail also has a connector trail to the park's other campground. This second campground juts off another side road with more beautiful spots for camping on Lake Russell. Both campgrounds have water and electric and many sites accommodate large RVS up to 30 or 49 feet. Campers can watch the sun rise over the lake on many sites.

A final side road leads down to a community building with a large parking area and an interesting playground built on several levels. This nice building with long windows and outdoor decks can be rented for group meetings, reunions, and other occasions. It has a kitchen area and bathrooms and access to the lake but is private for group gatherings. Calhoun Falls is a lovely lakeside park, ideal for family getaways.

For history buffs, nearby Abbeville, only 18 miles and approximately 30 minutes from the park, is a quaint, charming town full of historic architecture. The picturesque Abbeville square has shops, boutiques, restaurants a theatre and an opera house. Festivals and concerts are often hosted in the city plus a live concert series. The Burt-Stark Mansion whispers of the Civil War era, with its beautiful antebellum home and grounds, as do other historic homes around town and several Confederate era churches.

Sadlers Creek State Park

Upstate - Anderson County
Park Address: 940 Sadlers Creek Rd, Anderson, SC 29626
Park Size: 395 acres   Month Visited: October
Directions: From I-26 take I-85 west past the Greenville exits and turning south on Hwy 29 at Piedmont. Follow Hwy 29 past Anderson exits to Hwy 187 north and then left at 741/Shelter Cove Road and into the park.

Park Description:

　　　　Sadlers Creek State Park sits on a picturesque peninsula jutting out into Lake Hartwell. The 56,000-acre reservoir borders Georgia and South Carolina with 963 miles of shoreline. The park offers camping, fishing, boating, and hiking. The lake and the nearby Hartwell Dam were named for Revolutionary War heroine Nancy Hart. A tough, feisty and resourceful frontier woman, she often outsmarted British soldiers, helping the Revolutionary cause, and Native Ameri-

cans called her "Wahatche" or War Woman.

As in many other lakeside parks in South Carolina, the visitor center and park office can be found inside the park on the waterfront rather than near the park entrance. After entering the park, follow the signs to the center at the back of a scenic loop road. The park office and large pavilion sit on a rise in front of Lake Hartwell

with a broad covered deck across the back that looks out across the lake. Near the office and pavilion are picnic areas, a children's playground, and a horseshoe pit, as well as access to one of the park's hiking trails.

The 0.5-miles Pine Grove Trail, a nice paved walkway winds from the back of the parking area and loops through the woods, providing an easy walking trail for all ages and abilities. Alongside the trail is the park's 9-hole disc golf course. Frisbees for the course can be attained at the park office, as can loaner rods and reels. The park offers a variety of educational and fun programs during the year for visitors like the Fall Family Fun Day.

Up the road from the pavilion and office, a side road leads down to a beautiful fishing pier on the lake. This long pier provides a great place to fish on a quiet cove. Lake Hartwell is famous for great fishing, with a fine habitat for striped bass, walleye, bream and catfish, and many professional bass tournaments are held on the lake. A drive all the way to the end of the main park road leads to a primitive campground area for group camping and to one of the park's pub-

lic campground areas. Sadlers Creek offers two nice campgrounds with a total of 52 standard campsites with water and electric, restroom facilities, and a dump station, along with 14 sites for tent camping. Near the group camping area are two access points to the 6-mile biking and hiking trail that winds through the park. The dirt trail follows orange markers winding its way through the forest and along the lake.

Returning to the main road, another side road leads down to the park's

boat ramp. There is a boat pier, a large parking lot and a wide level ramp where boating and fishing enthusiasts can put in their boats for a day on the lake. The final road before leaving the park leads to the park's second campground area.Two loop roads provide nice campground spaces for tents and RVs with restrooms and a dump station. This campground area has a large recreation pavilion, a ballfield, basketball courts, a beautiful children's playground and access to the lake for fishing and swimming. The park biking and hiking trail winds in and out at several points, too, for walks or bike rides into the woods.

Although small, Sadlers Creek State Park is especially pretty and it is also close to many nearby sites for day trips. In Anderson, only 14 miles away there are restaurants and shopping malls. Downtown is

Carolina Wren Park that hosts free concerts and has a splash pad for kids and nearby is the award-winning Anderson County Museum with programs and exhibits. Outside of Anderson is the Split Creek dairy and cheese farm with tours and a farm store. In Clemson, 25.6 miles from the park is the South Carolina Botanical Gardens with 295 acres of gardens, trails, and a lake, free to the public and open all seasons. Also several historic homes can be visited in the area—Hanover House built in 1716 and on the National Register of Historic Places, Hopewell Plantation, and Fort Hill, the antebellum plantation home of John C. Calhoun.

Lake Hartwell State Park

Upstate - Oconee County
Park Address: 19138 SC Hwy 11, Fair Play, SC 29643
Park Size: 680 acres   Month Visited: October
Directions: From I-26, take I-85 west past the Greenville, Anderson, and Clemson exits to turn north on Cherokee Foothills Scenic Highway #11 to park entrance on left.

Park Description:

Lake Hartwell State Park is in a very accessible location to Interstate 85 on the Georgia and South Carolina border, making this park busy year round and its campground frequently full to capacity. The Friday we visited before a Clemson University football game weekend, the campground was packed and the "full" sign displayed at the park entrance. Created in 1976, the Lake Hartwell park offers fourteen miles of shoreline, fine opportunities for fishing and boating, picnicking, camping, and hiking.

The park visitor center, on the right just past the park entrance sign, is a beautiful facility with a gift shop and store, a small museum, space for park programs, and an outdoor deck with benches and picnic tables flanked by flowers and attractive landscaping. The museum offers displays telling the park's history and showing wildlife found in the area and it has a collection of vintage fish-

ing equipment and a fish tank with native species. On a hillside by the visitor center is a paved basketball court and the park's large group picnic shelter that can accommodate groups up to 75. On the left beyond the visitor center is the trailhead for the Beech Bluff Trail, marked with a wooden sign by the road reading "Nature Trail." The trail winds back into the woods and to a small, secluded lake. This easy to moderate in-and-out hiking trail is approximately three-fourths miles in length, or 1.5-miles roundtrip. Because the trail loops around to end further up the main park road, hikers can hike back on the paved road to the parking area if they prefer.

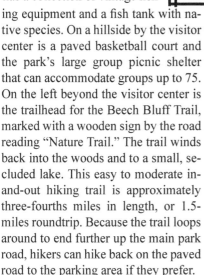

The road to the left before the visitor center winds down to a picturesque day use area on a beautiful peninsula on the lake. There are lakeside picnic tables and benches here, a children's playground, a boat ramp, and a long 140-foot fishing pier reaching out into a quiet cove. We saw several families enjoying the wide lakeside shoreline in this area, which makes a nice spot for swimming or kayaking. Near the beginning of the park's campground area is a second boat dock situated on another peaceful cove off the

main lake. Life jackets are available for loan here as is a courtesy dock. The fishing is excellent on Lake Hartwell with striped bass, smallmouth bass, walleye, largemouth bass, bream and catfish. Many bass tournaments are held on Lake Hartwell each year like the Bassmaster Classic.

Lake Hartwell State Park offers a total of 115 paved campsites in its campground area at the end of the main park road, many which can accommodate large RVs up to 40 feet. There are also thirteen tent sites, most waterfront in quiet spots. The large campground has three different camping areas, each on fingers reaching out into Lake Hartwell. All sites have water and electric hookups and nearby restrooms with hot showers, and the park provides a dump station and a large trash dumpster. The park camping sites are all scenic, although somewhat small in comparison with other parks, and the paved roads into and around the campground areas are somewhat rutted, winding and narrow. Many of the camp spots sit on hillside sites with somewhat steep drives reaching down toward the lake so the park advises bringing leveling

equipment for campers and RVs. A detailed campground map of all sites is available at the park office to help campers and visitors find their way around this large campground.

In addition, the park offers two 12x12 foot rental cabins at the end of one of the campground peninsulas. Each rustic cabin has a double bed, bunks, a small front porch, and a lovely waterfront deck directly on the lake. The small cabins offer indoor light, heat and air, but no restrooms. However, a park restroom is located close to the cabins and each has a water spigot and fire ring outside for cooking and cleanup. The park also has plans to build more cabins in future for visitors who don't have campers or tents.

Convenient to the interstate, this state park is also close to South Carolina's mountain country further up the Cherokee Foothills National and Scenic Byway. Directly across the lake, 17 minutes away by car and less by boat, is Georgia's Tugaloo State Park with more fishing spots, several hiking trails and a fine sand swim beach. Not far away in Georgia are 186-foot Toccoa Falls and the Tallulah Gorge with six waterfalls and an interpretive center.

Cowpens National Battlefield Park

Upstate - Cherokee County
Park Address: 4001 Chesnee Hwy, Gaffney, SC 29341
Park Size: 845 acres   Month Visited: November
Directions: From I-26. follow Hwy 11/Chesnee Highway. After passing through Chesnee, continue on thru the intersection with Hwy 221/110 and then turn right on Piedmont Road which leads directly into the park.

Park Description:

Cowpens National Battlefield Park commemorates a pivotal battle fought in the American Revolutionary War. On January 17, 1781, Brigadier General Daniel Morgan led his soldiers in a swift and decisive victory over Lieutenant Colonel Banastre Tarleton's British regiment, proving to be an important victory. The battle turned the tide in the war, boosting American morale and causing the British to lose control of South Carolina and leading to the British defeat eight months later. The Revolutionary War began when the Thirteen Colonies in America declared independence from Great Britain on July 1776. The war waged between the Patriots and Loyalists from April 19, 1775, through October 19, 1781 until British General Cornwallis surrendered at Yorktown. The war officially ended on September 3, 1783, when The Treaty of Paris was signed, in Paris, France, by King George III of Great Britain and representatives of the brand new United States of America.

The park, with free entry, is open seven days a week, 9:00 am – 5:00 pm, except for holidays. The Cowpens Revolutionary War battle site has a visitor center and museum, a picnic area and camping area, and either walking trails or an auto loop road for touring the battlefield. The best place to begin a visit is at the visitor center. In the sidewalk leading to the visitor center are commemorative plaques and in front of the center is the tall U.S. Memorial Monument. Dedicated in 1932, the monument recognizes all the men who fought at the Battle of Cowpens. Inside the visitor center behind the monument, a wealth of information about the war and battle can be attained, including maps and brochures. The visitor center also has a fine museum with an 18-minute film about the Battle

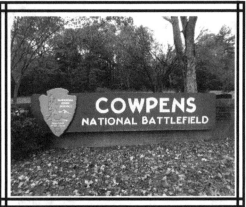

of Cowpens, exhibits, weapons, a 300-lb cannon, and a 13-minute fiber-optic map display that illustrates battle sites and tactics. The park holds a multitude of special events throughout the year including guided battlefield walks, calvary and musket demonstrations and artillery events, 18th century music concerts, history talks, children's activities and outdoor dramas. The park also hosts a Fourth of July celebration, a yearly anniversary celebration and living history days and weekends.

Behind the visitor center is a sign at the beginning of the one-mile Battlefield Trail. We enjoyed walking this self-guided trail with kiosks along the way to explain the points of interest the trail passed. The brochure and battlefield map we picked up in the visitor center provided more information. This was an easy, level paved trail to walk and especially pretty with fall color along the way. Points on the trail included the Washington Light Infantry Monument, notes about Morgan's army, pictorials of the battle at different points, and a few rest benches.

75

Returning back to the center we then drove the three-mile loop road around the perimeter of the battlefield. Along the way, you can stop at different places to walk in to see monuments or points of interest. One stop even gave an explanation of how cow pastures had turned into a battlefield. Midway around the loop road is a pavilion, picnic area and small camping area. The two-mile Cowpens Nature Trail can be found here, also, for a walk through the woods and back to a small stream.

Continuing on the loop road, there are pullover parking spots at the Green River Road, also a nice trail to walk. A short distance away is a cutoff road to the historic Robert Scruggs House. The cabin was built in 1828 by an early settler. Robert and his wife Catharine farmed the acreage around the cabin and raised a family of eleven children. The cabin and land around it stayed in the family until the mid-1970s when the National Park Service purchased the land, later restoring the cabin more to its original appearance.

Further along the loop road are side roads to two more battlefield sites with explanation plaques and short walks you can take linking into the Green River Road and and to parts of the Battlefield Trail again. The Green River Road, passing directly through the battlefield park, ran from the Pacolet River in South Carolina to the Green River and on into North Carolina. Later in history, the Overmountain Men traveled the Green River Road and through Cowpens to battle the British at Kings Mountain.

History Note:
Brigadeer General Daniel Morgan (1736-1802) was a brilliant strategic military leader and also had a colorful history. Born in New Jersey, one of seven children, he left home at 17, moving to Virginia and eventually building a thriving teamster business. He served as a civilian teamster, along with his cousin Daniel Boone, in the French and Indian War, coining his later military nickname "The Old Waggoner." Morgan had an early disdain for the British and their rule and received a severe punishment of lashes for attacking a British officer. This was usually a fatal sentence, but Morgan survived, and was quick to join in the militia when the Revolutionary War began. Despite a somewhat rebellious regard for authority, often causing him disciplinary action, Morgan's continued bravery, military skill, and ability to inspire his men, led to multiple promotions and eventually to the rank of Brigadeer General under Nathanael Green. Green sent Morgan to harass the enemy in the backcountry of South Carolina but British General Cornwallis soon sent Colonel Banastre Tarleton to track him down. Although Morgan hadn't been given orders to engage in direct battle, he set up a direct, well-planned confrontation anyway, helping to turn the tide of the war. For his actions, he received lands in Virginia and later built a large estate and home there, named Saratoga. Morgan also served in the U.S. House of Representatives.

Battle of Musgrove Mill State Historic Site

Upstate - Union County
Park Address: 398 State Park Road, Clinton, TN 29325
Park Size: 44 acres   Month Visited: November
Directions: From I-26, take Exit 52 for Cross Anchor/Clinton, turning east on Hwy 56. Follow 56 north toward Cross Anchor about six miles to park entrance on left.

Park Description:

  This state park marks the historic site where the Revolutionary War Battle of Musgrove Mill took place on August 19, 1780. The property once be-

longed to Major Edward Musgrove, who operated a prosperous mill at Horseshoe Bend on the Enoree River and owned a large plantation house on the hillside nearby. During the war the British took control of Musgrove's property due to its advantageous situation and mill. While the British were encamped at this site, Patriot leader Colonel Isaac Shelby and a militia of Overmountain Men thought the British forces small enough to defeat. However, as the battle began, they learned 300 additional British soldiers had joined the encampment, traveling from Ninety-Six. Although outnumbered two to one, the Patriots battled fiercely before retreating, suffering only four casualties compared to hundreds lost by the British. The valiant battle signaled the strength of the Patriot forces and helped to begin turning the tide of the Patriot war effort in South Carolina.

  At the large park visitor and interpretive center you can learn more about the Battle of Musgrove Mill, the Revolutionary War, and the history of the area. The center, open 10-4 weekdays and 10-5 weekends, has an information center, a museum and a small store with books, souvenirs, and period crafts. Near the visitor center one of the park's two trails begins beside a large picnic pavilion. The one-mile British Camp Trail loops through the woods and along the banks of the Enoree River before curling back to the parking area again. Along the route are historic markers and the Mary Musgrove Monument. This

rock monument is dedicated to one of Major Edward Musgrove's daughters, who legends claim aided the Patriots during the Revolutionary battle and helped her sweetheart escape from the British. Past the monument, the trail winds through the woods and then turns to follow along the Enoree River. There are pretty scenes along the riverbank before the trail curls around to a picnic area on

Musgrove Mill Lake and to its end near the parking area. Both the lake and the Enoree River are popular for fishing and loaner rods and reels are available free at the park office.

The second part of this park lies across the Enoree River. With the old bridge gone, you need to drive to this section of the park. Leaving the park, continue on Hwy 56, past a DAR historic marker and across the Enoree River bridge, to Horseshoe Falls Road on the left. Follow this road to a parking area and park sign. You will find the 1.7-miles Battlefield Trail, sometimes called the Horseshoe Falls Trail, just past the parking lot on the left before the green bridge. The first 100 yards of the trail is paved and handicap accessible and leads to pretty Horseshoe Falls. The falls is a delightful cascade spreading all the way across the river with giant rocks and lovely spots for wading. Beyond the falls the trail continues on through the woods to the historic battle site before looping around to return. The entire trail is cool and pleasant with historic markers, bridges, steps, big holly trees and benches along the way. Don't miss seeing both sections of this interesting state park that is on the National Register of Historic Places.

Rose Hill Plantation State Historic Site

Upstate - Union County
Park Address: 2677 Sardis Road, Union, SC 29379
Park Size: 44 acres   Month Visited: November
Directions: From I-26, exit at Clinton onto Hwy 72 east. Turn left
at Whitmire on Hwy 176 and then take a quick left again onto Old
Buncombe Road. Follow Buncombe to Sardis Road on the right.
Continue on Sardis, staying right when it merges into State Rd 44,
following north to the park entrance.

Park Description:

     Rose Hill Plantation, on the National Register of Historic Places, pre-
serves the home site of an early South Carolina landowner and governor. William
Henry Gist (1807-1874) was the 68th Governor of South Carolina and he was a
strong leader in the secession movement, signing the Ordinance of Secession
in 1860, which launched the Confederacy and the War Between the States. Gist
came to Union County as a young child and when his father died soon after, he
was taken in and later adopted by his uncle. He studied law as a young man, established a practice in the Union County area and built Rose Hill Plantation on
land his father had left him. Gist was a prosperous landowner and his plantation
home, maintained by a small army of slaves, once covered over 6000 acres. In
1828 Gist married Louisa Bowen, who later died at eighteen after giving birth to
their second child. He remarried in 1832 to Mary Rice and they had 12 children,

although only four survived to adulthood. In 1840 Gist was elected to the SC House of Representatives and then to the Senate in 1844 for three terms. In 1858 he became the Governor of South Carolina and his home at Rose Hill served as the Governor's Mansion.

William Gist's plantation home is interesting to visit and you first see the main house, in all its grandeur, after driving down a long tree-lined lane from the main road. The stately two and one-half storied Georgian style home, set amid old magnolia trees and manicured gardens, is the center point of this small historic park. The grounds are open daily 9-6, but you can only see the interior of the plantation home at set tour times, so be sure to check the park schedule for days and times before planning your visit. The house tour is a treat—and shouldn't be missed—as this old plantation home has been beautifully preserved and is full of period furniture, old portraits, a bust of Governor Gist, and a wealth of historic artifacts. The main rooms downstairs are especially impressive, showing the wealth of the era with green paint in the dining room, rare except among the rich, and a piano in the living area across the hallway. The tour also takes you upstairs to see the grand ballroom, family bedrooms, and a view from one of the wide exterior porches.

Around the grounds are outbuildings, a caretaker's house, an old log home, and picturesque garden pathways passing neatly trimmed hedges, flower gardens, and the rose bushes the plantation was named after. Inside the old brick kitchen house directly behind the main plantation home is the park office, a small museum, and a gift shop. Near the carriage house and parking lot is a shaded picnic area with tables and a picnic shelter that can be rented for events. Below the picnic area a kiosk notes where the beginning of a short 0.5-miles Nature Trail begins. The trail winds through the woods and comes out on the plantation home's back lawn. Branching off the Nature Trail is a turn to the longer 2.0-mile River Trail, which winds down to the Tyger River and back.

Croft State Park

Upstate - Spartanburg County
Park Address: 450 State Park Rd, Spartanburg, SC 29302
Park Size: 7,054 acres   Month Visited: November
Directions: From I-26, take Exit 22, go east on Hwy 296 appx one mile and turn onto Hwy 295 until it intersects with Hwy 56. Turn right on Hwy 5 and then left on Dairy Ridge Road for less than a half mile to the park sign and entrance.

Park Description:

Croft State Park, less than ten miles outside of Spartanburg, is a vast park with a wide variety of recreational activities including boating, fishing, camping, tennis courts, a bocce ball court, and multitudes of trails for hiking, biking, and horseback riding. Rich with history, the area was once home to early settlers and later the site of a World War II Army Training and prisoner-of-war camp. On the grounds are a Revolutionary War site, remains of a popular old resort, Whitestone Springs, built around a local spring, the remnants of an old mill, and seven historic cemeteries.

To begin exploring the park, drive in the main entrance and follow the park road almost to its end, stopping at the park office. Although the park is open daily, the office is only open 11am–Noon and 4-5pm. There are usually park maps and brochures in a rack by the door, but we'd advise bringing a map from the state park web site to help find your way around this large and spread out park.

Near the park office is a recreational area with picnic tables, a large picnic shelter, and a playground. The park has three shelters that can be rented for gatherings and near the office is one of the park's two campground areas. Both campground areas, with 50 total sites, are on scenic, shaded loop roads with water and electric, with sites for large RVs up to 40 feet, restrooms, hot showers, and a dump station. In addition, the park has a primitive group camping area for up to a hundred. The park has a large swimming pool, too, but it was closed at the time of this writing.

Directly behind the park office is a fine equestrian center that Croft State Park is renown for around the southeast. It has a large well-maintained horse show arena and stands, a practice ring, 54 rental horse stalls, and a large parking area for

trucks and horse trailers. Every third Saturday, from February through November, the Spartanburg Horseman's Association holds a horse show at the equestrian center from 9am – 6pm with events for jumping, English, gaited, Western, and many more classifications. The park also has 24 miles of equestrian trails, most accessible from the equestrian center, making this a favorite recreational area for all who love to ride.

For bikers, Croft has a fine network of ten biking trails covering over 20 miles, ideal for mountain bike riding. The trails are clearly marked on the park's trail map and signs designate which trails are open to bikers. The mountain biking trails can be accessed

from the main recreation area or from a Southside Parking lot on the southeastern boundary of the park. The Southside area also has a SCDNR Skeet Shooting Range for skeet, rifles, pistols, and archery.

Hikers can hike on all trails, but there are several trails designated for hiking only. We explored several of the hiking trails on our visit. A short memorable trail for anyone visiting the park is the half-mile Palmetto Trail, which starts not far from the park office off the main road. The trail is an easy in and out walk leading through the woods and down to beautiful Fairforest Creek. There are rest benches here along the creekside and visitors can walk across the 65-foot Advance America expansion bridge, the longest foot bridge in the South Carolina state park system. At the creek you can wade in the water, rock hop over large boulders in the creek, or explore the trail further across the bridge, which leads by old homesteads.

Less than a block from the beginning of the Palmetto Trail another nice 1.5-miles Nature Trail begins between two fence posts and is clearly marked. This trail is a loop trail through the woods and down to the creek, also, but passes rock remains of the old Foster Mill which once operated in the area. Along the way on this trail, too, are signs identifying the different trees and telling interesting facts about them.

We also enjoyed hiking pieces of the Foster Mill Loop trail to see the historic bridge at Kelsey Creek near where a Revolutionary Battle was fought and walking the short trail piece to the old Foster Cemetery. This entire park is latticed with lovely trails and we wished we'd had time to hike and explore more.

While at the park, don't miss driving down the side road by the park office to beautiful, blue 165-acre Lake Craig. The second campground is off this road with a boat ramp and scenic point at the road's end. We loved walking out on the big fishing pier here and alongside the river on a boardwalk by the boathouse, where visitors can rent fishing boats, canoes, kayaks, and stand-up paddleboards. Private boats are permitted, too, but only with electric trolling motors. This is a beautiful spot with an 0.75-miles short hiking trail, rest benches, and lovely views out over the lake.

To get to the park's other smaller lake, Lake Johnson, leave the park via the main park road, turn right on Daisy Ridge Road, and then right on Whitestone Road/295 for approximately two miles to Lake Johnson Road on the right. At the end of this road is the scenic lake, with good fishing for bass, bream, and other fish. There is a boat ramp at the lake, good fishing spots on the lakeside, and a picnic pavilion on the hillside. A nice hiking trail is easily accessible at the park, the 1.5-miles Lake Johnson Trail that winds around the lakeside. We enjoyed watching anglers on our visit to this section of the park and while sitting on a park bench we watched two men flying remote controlled airplanes. All in all this is a beautiful and interesting state park that is a gem to visit. Don't miss it when you are in this part of South Carolina.

Chester

MIDLANDS SOUTH CAROLINA STATE PARK INDEX

MIDLANDS
South Carolina
PARKS

Kings Mountain

Wateree

Barnwell

Aiken

Kings Mtn National Military Park

Midlands - York/Cherokee Counties
Park Address: 2625 Parks Rd, Blacksburg, SC 29702
Park Size: 294 acres   Month Visited: November
Directions: From I-26, take I-85 northeast at Spartanburg, follow through Blacksburg and then turn right/south onto Hwy 216/Battleground Road into Park.

Park Description:

Kings Mountain National Military Park preserves the site of the Revolutionary War Kings Mountain battle of October 7, 1780, an important American victory in the fight for independence from Great Britain. Thomas Jefferson called this battle "the turning of the tide of success." The battle was fought entirely by irregular American Loyalists and British forces led by their Commander Major Patrick Ferguson.

The park is open seven days a week, 9:00 am – 5:00 pm, except for holidays and admittance is free. As with most state and national parks, the best place to begin your exploration of the park is at the visitor center. It sits in a scenic spot on a hillside, with a picnic area on the grounds, and the area was rich with fall color at our visit in November. The park visitor center is large with an information center, gift shop and bookstore, exhibits, artifacts, a wealth of paintings, and a museum. The museum has been uniquely designed so visitors can walk through an exhibit created to resemble the landscape of the 1780 battlefield.

Along the way are audio and visual exhibits to teach the history of the battle and the commanders, leaders, and men who fought in it. There is also a 25-minute film about the 1780 battle you can take time to watch.

Behind the visitor center, you can begin a 1.5-miles loop hike on a paved asphalt walkway past scenes in the Kings Mountain battle with markers and informative placards along the way to explain sites you encounter. The Battlefield Trail sign has an arrow pointing to the right to suggest the direction to follow on this trail, but for an easier more downhill, instead of mostly uphill hike, we suggest walking to the left on this loop trail rather than to the right. Additionally, if you do not have time or stamina to hike the entire trail, by walking to the left for about a quarter of a mile, you will soon come to the two main monuments on this battlefield trail and then can turn around and return, having enjoyed an interesting portion of the overall hike.

Following right as the sign suggests, the trail winds gradually downhill at first, passing several placards and a few gravesites to an area along the creek. The markers detail how the forest environment was beneficial to the American Patriots, most fighting with only long rifles, and offer interesting information about the battle. Grave markers along the pathway give names of some of the men who died in the battle like Captain John Mattocks, and soldier silhouettes depict battle scenes. As the walkway drops to the creek, there is one of several benches placed along the trail for a rest stop. The trail then passes the Old Colonial Road that the American

Patriots followed into Kings Mountain. After this point the walkway rises and climbs continually for over a mile up the ridge side of the mountain passing

more markers and a spring before reaching a side trail to the Hoover Monument. On October 7, 1930, President Herbert Hoover came to visit Kings Mountain National Military Park to help commemorate the 150th anniversary of the battle. He addressed an audience of about 75,000 people. The park was thronged with visitors for the event and a special bandstand was created where the president gave his anniversary address. A year later the Daughters of the American Revolution Kings Mountain Chapter erected a rock monument to memorialize the location where Hoover gave his speech and you can see the monument at the end of this side trail.

Curling around to the top of the hill, after passing the Hoover Monument site, the trail arrives at the Centennial Monument, a 28-foot granite pylon atop five gradated granite steps that was dedicated in 1980. Inscriptions commemorate patriotic Americans who fought in the Battle of Kings Mountain. Not far from the Centennial Monument is another taller granite monument, The United States Monument. At 83-feet in height, it rests on a two-step marble base, with bronze tablets on each side of the monument dedicated to the Patriot victory. The final walkway section across the hilltop passes the spot where Ferguson fell, his forces soon defeated, and where he was later buried, and then winds downhill back to the visitor center.

History Note:

The Battle of Kings Mountain only lasted for 65 minutes, due to the good strategy, courage, and skill of the American Loyalists, many of whom were Overmountain Men. The Overmountain Men were not regular militia but frontiersmen, most from west of the Appalachian Mountains of North Carolina and what is now Tennessee, Kentucky, and southwest Virginia. The term "over

mountain" arose from the men being from "over" the geographic boundary between the 13 American colonies and the western frontier. In response to Ferguson's threats toward their homes and lives, these men responded by creating an irregular militia, determined to cross the mountains to defeat Ferguson first. The men gathered at the fort at Symamore Shoals, in what is now Elizabethton, TN, to march south together on what is now known as The Overmountain Trail, adding other units as they headed south. Learning Ferguson had camped on the ridgetop at Kings Mountain on his way to join Cornwallis at Charlotte, the Patriot group circled in, split and surrounded the ridge camp, and then attacked. The pluck and bravery of these men is legend and today re-enactments fo the battle are held at the park to remember this famous victory.

PhotoCredit: Pam Mulinix

Kings Mtn State Park

Midlands - York County
Park Address: 1277 Park Rd, Blacksburg, SC 29702
Park Size: 6,885 acres   Month Visited: November
Directions: From I-26, take I-85 northeast at Spartanburg, follow through Blacksburg and then turn right/south onto Hwy 216 Battleground Road which leads through Kings Mtn National Military Park and into Kings Mtn State Park or follow I-85 to Hwy 161. Turn south and enter park on Park Road/Hwy 705.

Park Description:

The Kings Mountain National Military Park and the Kings Mountain State Park have adjoining properties so you can easily enjoy visiting both parks on the same day. Information about Kings Mountain State Park and a park map can be picked up at the small Park Office just inside the west Park Entrance or at the Trading Post camp store near the campground. Kings Mountain State Park has a vast acreage of 6,885 acres but only a part of it is developed for recreational enjoyment. The rest is wilderness, latticed with hiking and equestrian trails and scenic forest.

After picking up park information at the small Park Office just inside the east entrance on Park Road, backtrack and turn on Lake Crawford Road to head to the park's main recreation area. As you drive in, you will pass scenes of 13-acres Lake Crawford and soon arrive at a fine recreational area and play-

ground on a hillside. There are picnic pavilions, public restrooms, and a picnic area here, with a large recreation building across the street. Just beyond the parking area as you enter the campground there is a cute Trading Post and Park Store on the hillside with a rock patio in front of it. Open from March to November, the store offers tourist information, maps, and limited supplies and grocery needs. The large campground behind the Trading Post has 115 camping sites for RV or tent camping along several winding, interconnected roads. Several sites will accommodate RVs up to 40 feet and there are also ten additional rustic tent sites on a side road. Within the campground are basketball and volleyball courts, a dump station, restrooms, showers and dumpsters.

Across the street from the recreational area and campground, and behind the recreational building, is pretty Lake Crawford. Several trails lead down to the lake and along the lakeside, and there are many fine fishing sites along this beautiful lake. A trail following down wooden stairs leads to a nice hiking trail that winds across a bridge over Clark Ford Creek with views of the dam at one end of Lake Crawford. The trail winds left behind the lake and also branches into other park trails, like the 16-mile long Kings Mountain Trail winding throughout the park. There are over 30 miles of trails in the park to explore. Swimming is not

allowed at the lake but canoes, kayaks, and jon boats without motors can use the lake, either brought in or rented from the park.

Not far beyond the park office on the main park road another side road, Camp Cherokee Road, leads to two group camps. When the road splits the left fork leads back to the YMCA Cherokee Group Camp, established in 1945 for children six to fifteen, and the right fork leads to the park's own York Group Camp. We followed the right fork when the road split to drive to the end of the road to see this group camp area, which had a large rustic lodge and cabins. Along the road leading back to the York Camp is an access road leading down to an entry point where visitors can put boats into a side creek that leads out into Lake York. We could not see the lake from this small boat launch area or from the road or group camp, but photos show that it is a huge 65-acre lake hidden in the backwoods of the park. Only non-motorized craft are allowed on the lake and no swimming is allowed except at the YMCA camp area. But canoers, kayakers, and anglers love this big lake not readily accessible to the general public. For the adventurous, a few rough trails lead down to the lake's banks here and there, but none are marked or well-maintained by the park. So don't be disappointed if you don't see this lake at all on your visit to the Kings Mountain State Park. As a historic note of interest, both park lakes were built and created by the Civilian Conservation Corps (CCC) and you can see their handiwork in other areas of the park, too, in old cabins, rock walls, and structures.

As you head back out of the group camp area, stop to get out of your car to explore the Living History Farm, one of the special aspects of this state park. The farm is a replica of a mid 19th century Piedmont Farm. At the parking area, follow the wooded walkway back into the farm grounds. You will soon come to an old cabin, outhouse, and other farm buildings. As you walk around the farm property you will find barns, a cotton gin, a blacksmith, sheds, a weave shop, beehives, a garden plot, and farm animals in the fenced field. Kiosks and placards provide information about the different points within the farm and tell about the farm site's history. Ranger-led programs are often given at the farm and old-time demonstrations and special programs are offered on the grounds. In addition, a 1.5-miles hiking trail connects the farm site to the recreational area.

Further up the main park road, heading toward the boundary with the Kings Mountain National Military Park, a turning at Apple Road leads into the park's Equestrian Camp. This campsite offers special features to accommodate campers who bring horses. There are 15 equestrian camping sites here, a large day use equestrian parking area, and access to over 15 miles of equestrian trails.

If you camp at Kings Mountain State Park or stay in the area, you might want to also explore the Crowders Mountain State Park just across the border in North Carolina. The two parks are only about four miles apart. Crowders Mountain State park is a 5,210-acre park, and includes the peaks of Crowder's Mountain and the The Pinnacle with many of its fine hiking trails climbing to stunning vistas and summits.

Andrew Jackson State Park

Midlands - Lancaster County
Park Address: 196 Andrew Jackson Park Rd, Lancaster, SC 29720
Park Size: 360 acres   Month Visited: November
Directions: From I-77, exit at Rock Hill on Hwy 21 and follow to Hwy 5. As Hwy 5 ends, swing left briefly onto Old Church Road to cross railroad tracks to Hwy 521. Turn left and drive north on Hwy 521 appproximately one half mile to park sign on right.

Park Description:

Andrew Jackson State Park, although small, offers a combination of historic sites, activities, picnic areas, walking trails, a campground, and an 18-acre lake. Established to honor the seventh U.S. President Andrew Jackson, the park is a popular visitor destination.

After entering the park, drive to the end of the main road until it deadends into a parking lot. Walk up the sidewalk by the parking lot to the visitor center, which is in a building that looks like a split-level brown house. Inside the visitor center is an information center, gift shop, and a small museum dedicated to Andrew Jackson's memory. The museum interior includes a rustic room with a fireplace, wood walls, table, bed and other artifacts created to resemble Jackson's 18th Century early home, while a second room contains memorabilia and artifacts. Behind the visitor center is a fenced herb garden with an assortment of herbs used for cooking, medicine and dyeing in Jackson's day. Be aware that the visitor center and museum have limited visitor hours, open Saturday and Sunday 1:00 pm-5:00

pm and only by appointment on Monday through Friday.

Next to the visitor center stop to look at the old schoolhouse, a historic replica of an 18th Century one, much like Andrew Jackson might have attended, even with an old school bell on a post near the door. Across the parking lot from the schoolhouse is one of the park's large pavilions, this one rustic in appearance with a

big rock fireplace at one end. Behind the pavilion is a picnic area, a shady walking area, and the park's amphitheater. The large, scenic 7,500-sq ft wooden amphitheater is ideal for outdoor concerts, plays and weddings and sits in a pretty wooded setting.

Toward the back end of the parking lot, a walkway leads to a charming Meeting House, that looks somewhat like an old church building with another picnic area beside it. The Meeting House, which will seat up to 60 and has a kitchenette, can be rented from the park for small events. Beside the Meeting House is the beginning of one of the park's short walking trails, the 1.1-miles Nature Trail, or Crawford Trail, which winds on an easy quiet loop walk through the woods and back to the trail's beginning.

Continuing up the walkway beyond the Meeting House, the sidewalk passes several family grave markers. One of the markers near the statue has the words of Andrew Jackson, given in 1824, confirming his birth at this park site, once the plantation of his Uncle James Crawford. Andrew's father died before he was born and after his father's death, his mother and two brothers, Hugh and Robert, stayed alternately with two of Jackson's uncles, who helped to raise

him and his brothers. The homes of both uncles weren't far apart but later when the survey lines for North Carolina and South Carolina were drawn, the two uncles' properties fell on either side of the line. Jackson claimed to have been born on the South Carolina side at his Uncle James Crawford's plantation but some dispute that claim and say Jackson was born at his other uncle George McKerney's home three miles over the North Carolina line. Both states have markers and statues to Jackson's memory. It's a long-standing argument between the states. However, according to Jackson, he claimed verbally and in writing, and in his last will and testament, that he was a native born South Carolinian.

Just beyond the park markers is the stunning Anna Hyatt Huntington statue of a young Andrew Jackson on horseback. Equestrian statues were a specialty of the world-renowned sculptress, who with her husband Archer, founded Brookgreen Gardens in South Carolina where many of her works are displayed. When in her nineties, Huntington created this 10-ft tall, 25,000 lb bronze statue to commemorate the 200th anniversary of Andrew Jackson's birthday but didn't live to see its dedication. The statue named "Andrew Jackson – Boy of the Waxhaws" is a highlight of the park.

Leaving the historic area of the park, look for a second road nearer the entrance to head to the park's recreation and camping area. Shortly up the road, a side road off to the left winds down to one end of the 18-acre man-made lake. There is a boat ramp here where small non-motorized craft—fishing boats, canoes, and kayaks—can be put in. These boats can be brought in by visitors or rented from the park by the day. There is a nice parking area here, a handicapped fishing pier, a picnic area, and the beginning of the 1-mile Garden of the Waxhaws

Trail which winds around the park's lake. The trail is a moderately easy one, well-marked, with beautiful lake views and a rest bench along the way. It leads over a grassy causeway, along the back of the lake to a primitive campground area, and then loops around below the larger park campground and recreation area. Along this pleasant family trail are markers identifying plants and trees, with wild-flowers abundant along the trailside in spring.

At the park's main campground area are 25 campsites on gravel sites that will accommodate RVs up to 30 feet, including five paved sites for RVs up to 36 feet. The campground has restrooms, hot showers, electric and water, and a dump station. There are also a nice children's playground, horseshoe pits, a volleyball court, a picnic area and another pavilion. The campground and recreational area are picturesque and well maintained, nice for walking and biking and this is a pleasant family park.

History Note:

Andrew Jackson (1767-1845) called "Old Hickory" was one of America's early presidents and the last president who served in the Revolutionary War. His father died shortly before his birth, his mother and brothers during the Revolutionary War. Raised by his uncles, he studied law, was admitted to the bar in 1787, and soon moved to the frontier settlement of Nashville, TN, where he practiced law and became a wealthy landowner. Jackson, a member of the convention that established the TN Con-

stitution, was a respected military leader. He was elected to both the US House and Senate and served as President of the United States from 1829-1837. He married Rachel Donelson Robards and both are buried at The Hermitage, their plantation home outside Nashville which is open for public visits.

Landsford Canal State Park

Midlands - Chester County
Park Address: 2051 Park Drive, Catawba, SC 28704
Park Size: 448 acres   Month Visited: November
Directions: From I-77, exit at Rock Hill onto Hwy 21 and follow
to Hwy 327/Lansford Road. Turn east on 327/Lansford Road to
park entrance sign.

Park Description:

      This small park along the Catawba River offers natural beauty, unique trails, good fishing spots, and interesting historic sites. To begin your exploration, drive to the end of the first and main entrance road, staying right when the road splits, to a parking lot at a scenic recreation area along the river. Pretty in all seasons, this area has a small pavilion and picnic area, a children's playground, restrooms, lovely river views, and a rustic log cabin with a broad, covered front porch. The park office is located in the cabin but offers limited hours, only open from 11am to Noon. For this reason, you might want to read about the park's offerings prior to your visit and print your own park map to bring along.

      Where the main entrance road splits earlier, staying left instead of right leads up hill to a kiosk and the park's boat ramp for kayak and canoe enthusiasts. Beside the ramp runs one of the park's three trails, the short 0.25-miles Eagle Point Trail, which starts at the main picnic area and ends behind the park's museum, not visible from the road. This two-storied gray stone building was once the

Great Falls Canal lockkeeper's house. The museum has artifacts and pictorial displays but is only open to the public by appointment.

The highlight of the park, accessible to all on any day, are the 0.5-miles Nature Trail following the river and the 1.5-miles (3-miles RT) Canal Trail following the old tow path and canal beds of the Landsford Canal. Both of these trails begin just beyond the log house and picnic area at the same point. After a short distance the main trail splits, the Nature Trail continuing straight and the Canal Trail swinging to the right. If you follow the Nature Trail it travels along the river's edge, merging back into the Canal Trail at its end. You might spot herons, turtles, or eagles as you walk along and you'll find rest benches on this trail and an overlook near the trail's end. This pretty trail is especially popular from mid May until mid June when the rare, white Rocky Shoals Spider Lilies bloom in profusion for over twenty acres, drawing crowds of admirers.

The alternate Canal Trail follows through the woods along the tow path and canal beds of the old Landsford Canal the park is named for. In the 1820s, in order to get cotton shipments downriver to Charleston,

canals were built on the Catawba and Wateree rivers in areas where boats and barges couldn't get through dangerous rocky shoals easily. Of the four canals built only Landsford Canal still exists and it is on the National Historic Register. The canal, built by skilled and slave laborers, was a navigational channel created to bypass the rapids in the river, with five locks over a two-mile stretch. These locks raised and lowered the water levels as the barges passed through. It was fascinating to see the old stone canal walls, remnants of an old grist mill and the arched rock bridge at the Canal Trail's end. A second lockkeeper's house can be found at the end of the trail as well as a second park entrance allowing visitors to walk the canal trail from either end. Throughout the park are historic markers telling about interesting historical facts of the area.

Chester State Park

Midlands - Chester County
Park Address: 759 State Park Rd, Chester, SC 29706
Park Size: 523 acres   Month Visited: November
Directions: From I-77, take Hwy 9 to Chester, connecting to Hwy 72/West End Street south for approximately three miles to park sign and entrance.

Park Description:

The Chester State Park is a quiet, small, charming state park not far from Chester, South Carolina. The park was built in the 1930s as a Civilian Conservation Corps (CCC) project and many of the early buildings still stand. Chester is a scenic, shady, and peaceful park, built around a beautiful 160-acre lake. We found this small park to be a memorable gem in our journeys around the state. Within the park are a nice campground, a group camp area, a rustic meetinghouse, picnic areas and pavilions, playgrounds, a boat ramp, boathouse, walking trails, and a disc golf course.

As you enter the park, stop at the ranger station and camp office at a split in the road. This small rustic building is the first you will see after driving down a scenic winding road through the woods—especially pretty in the fall when the leaves have turned. The ranger station, only open from 11:00 am to Noon daily, has park maps, area information, and some items for sale like ice and treats. Beside the park office a side road leads to the park's campground on the lake. The campground has 25 sites for tents or RVs up to 40 feet, on a well-paved loop road, with nice restrooms, a bathhouse, a dump station, and dumpsters centrally located. This was really a nice campground for a small park and beautifully located. At the back of the campground several trails lead down to picnic tables and a fishing pier on the lake.

Returning to the main road, continue on the park's wooded drive, also great for biking, to a picturesque pavilion on a hillside, one of three pavilions in the park that can be rented for family or group gatherings. A larger facility, Lakeview Hall, can be found a short distance further down the road on a hillside looking over the lake. Lakeview Hall has a kitchen, pretty porches on the front and back and can accommodate up to 75 people.

The next side road beyond the meeting hall leads down to the park's boathouse. There is a boat ramp here for launching boats and other small craft with electric engines and there is also a second launch area with steps to the water for kayaks and canoes. Visitors can bring their own boats, or rent canoes, kayaks, paddleboats, and jon boats from the park for the day. This is a great lake for pleasure boating and fishing, and at the boathouse is a small fishing dock with a bench looking out across a panorama of the picturesque lake.

Beside the boathouse is the main access point to begin the 2.6-miles long Caney Fork Falls Trail that winds along the lakeside.

A sign with an arrow and the words Nature Trail note the beginning of the pathway. This easy family trail winds in and out along the side of the lake behind the meeting house and hillside pavilion to the campground area, where there is a second access point to the trail. The well-maintained path continues around to the back side of the lake to end at a dam and spillway at Caney Fork Creek, a nice spot for a rest before turning around to return.

Beyond the boathouse toward the back of the park is the main recreation area with two large rustic picnic pavilions and scenic picnic areas along the lakeside. There is an abundance of green space here for outdoor play and for lakeside fishing. You will also find two fabulous children's playgrounds. This area is a great family spot for a day on the lake. There is even a big patio with tables and benches, plus a covered pergola with swings where you can sit and dream while looking out over the sun-dappled lake views. In the middle of this pretty recreation area a 100-foot paved trail leads out to a long 450-foot bridge over the lake. You can enjoy nice views across the lake from the bridge and walk a trail along the lake on the other side. This park, although small, offers so many treats. You may see deer roaming freely, blue herons, ducks, turtles, birds, or beavers and a wide variety of wildflowers in the spring.

Chester State Park also has the first sanctioned South Carolina state park Disc Golf Course. The course was designed by Russell Schwarz and is suitable for professional and tournament play. The course has three loops with 27 holes and is well maintained. Moderately hilly, it is considered an advanced course but can also be played as a nine-hole short course for beginners.

Just beyond the disc golf course is a primitive group camping area with space for up to 50 in organized groups. The camping area has picnic tables, a fire ring, and isn't far from park restrooms.

For day trips while camping at Chester State Park, the park is only about thirty minutes from Landsford Canal State Park, a nearby historic site, and about 45 minutes from Lake Wateree State Park. Additionally, the town of Chester, the county seat of Chester County, is less than ten minutes away for trips to shop or to eat dinner out. The old Chester courthouse, built in 1852, is interesting to see and the town has several other notable buildings, like the old City Hall, Opera House and Kumler Hall, all on the National Register of Historic Places.

Redcliffe Plantation State Historic Site

Midlands - Aiken County
Park Address: 181 Redcliffe Rd, Beech Island, SC 29842
Park Size: 369 acres   Month Visited: August
Directions: From Interstate 20, exit on Hwy 1 south to Aiken to
Hwy 78 West. Follow Hwy 78 to Hwy 278 south through Beech
Island, then turn south on Hwy 580/Hammond Road for appx. 2
miles to Redcliffe Rd and into the park.

Park Description:

On the National Register of Historic Places, Redcliffe Plantation is a fine example of the lavish plantation estates built in South Carolina in the 1800s. The plantation, purchased in 1855, became the primary home of James Henry Hammond, his wife Catherine, and their eight children after their home was completed in 1859. The plantation stayed in the family for four generations and was last owned by John Shaw Billings, one of Hammond's great grandsons, who donated the property to the South Carolina State Park Service in 1973.

Today visitors can see the plantation property and take a 45-minute tour of the interior of the home, when it is open for tours. Not all the original buildings, that were a part of the old plantation, survived through the years but many did, showing well what this old home place and plantation was once like. On the property grounds, in addition to the large two-storied family home are also two old slave cabins, one now converted into a garage, a stable, historic gardens, a cistern, and beautiful old trees. A map, available at the visitor center, identifies all the buildings on the grounds. Another brochure identifies the wide diversity of trees on the property, including beautiful magnolias lining a roadway to the plantation house, giant oaks, mulberry, gardenia, catalpa, gingko, and others.

Redcliffe hosts many school tours and is a popular site for wedding events. The visitor center, when open, contains a gift shop and an interesting exhibit with old photos, documents, and information about the Hammond family and the plantation's earlier era. Redcliffe's story also includes the rich history of the African American families who once worked on the plantation as slaves and later as paid employees, tenant farmers, or sharecroppers, like the Goodwin, Wigfall, and Henley families.

Pictures and stories about these families can also be found in the exhibit center. If you miss the times when the center is open, you can find many photos and a wealth of information available on the Internet, too.

History Note:

Born near Newberry, SC, and the oldest of five children, James Henry Hammond (1807-1864) would rise to become a prominent landowner and well-known SC politician. After graduation from college, he established a successful law practice in Columbia. In 1831, he married a young heiress, Catherine Fitzsimmons, gained a large cotton plantation and property via marriage, and became a planter, later owning four plantations, in addition to Redcliffe, and hundreds of slaves. Hammond became a member of the SC House of Representatives from 1834-1836, Governor of SC from 1842-1844, and later a Senator from 1857-1860. Hammond was an ardent advocate for slavery and for secession. When the Civil War broke out in 1861,

he gave full support to the Confederate cause and two of his sons fought in the Confederacy. Despite his distinguished political career, Hammond's moral life was questionable and he was well known for repeated adulterous scandals. Hammond died at Redcliffe in 1864, just before the Civil War ended, and he was buried on the plantation's property.

Aiken State Park

Midlands - Aiken County
Park Address: 1145 State Park Rd, Windsor, SC 29856
Park Size: 1067 acres   Month Visited: August
Directions: From Interstate 20, take Hwy 1 south into Aiken, take
Hwy 78 East thru Montmorenci to Windsor. Coming in to Windsor, turn north on Hwy 53/State Park Road and follow to park.

Park Description:

  Just outside Aiken, SC, is the Aiken State Park. If you have time, stop to enjoy the city's charming downtown on your way to the park. Aiken is the largest city in the county, and you'll enjoy its old historic buildings, unique shops and restaurants, lovely gardens, fountains, and oak-lined streets like the famous South Boundary Avenue.

  Aiken State Park, established in 1934, was built during the years of the Great Depression, in part by an African-American division of the Civilian Conservation Corps (CCC), giving the park a unique legacy in its construction. Many of the buildings built by this detachment still remain in the park and an interpretive sign near the visitor center shares this history and shows a photo of these men who helped to create it. Aiken State Park is a large one, with 1067 acres, and the South Fork of the Edisto River runs directly through it. Many features make this park an interesting one to visit or to camp in.

  Begin your exploration by driving to the visitor center. The visitor

center office and gift shop are situated inside a large pavilion sitting on a hillside overlooking the lake. The pavilion is full of rustic chairs and picnic tables, making it a scenic spot. If you don't arrive during the hours when the center is open, you will still find maps and brochures outside the park office door. On the other side of the lake is a broad, shady recreation area containing two picnic pavilions, picnic tables,

a children's playground, and a roped off swim area. We ate our lunch in one of the pavilions, enjoying the day.

Continuing on the loop road beyond the visitor center, leads past a small pond and then to the campground. Around a shady road are 25 campsites with standard electric and water, restrooms with hot showers, and a dump station. The campground can accommodate small RVs and is also a great place for tent camping. At the back of the campground is one of the access points to the 3-mile Jungle Nature Trail that loops through the park. True to its name the trail winds through jungle-looking swampy, wetland areas and at one point crosses over a long boardwalk amid cypress trees. We'd advise spritzing with bug spray before hiking this trail and also you should keep an eye out for snakes.

Beyond the campground area a small side road leads back to Fishing Lake, another of Aiken's four lakes and ponds scattered around its grounds. This is a really pretty lake, well-loved for fishing, with water lilies clustered in several areas around its banks. A short walking bridge leads across a culvert to

a nice picnic area with tables and a pavilion. You will also see one of the park's rock artesian wells here near the pavilion, but you'll find a more spectacular artesian well further up the road. J.L. tried a little fishing here before we moved on, using a visitor's pole.

As the ongoing road loops around the park grounds it comes next to the Riverside Canoe Put-In Dock on the Edisto River. For water enthusiasts, the 1.7-miles canoe and kayak Water Trail that begins here is one of the most beloved features of this park. Beside the parking area, you will see canoes that can be rented from the park. In addition, kayaks and jon boats are also available for rent. A concrete ramp leads into the river and boaters can paddle down the Edisto to the trail's end where there is a second Take-Out Dock. Cypress trees are abundant here on this black water river and beside the path to the dock is another artesian well, spewing water so clean you can dip your hands in the cold spring water to drink it.

The ongoing park road then makes its way to the Cypress Stump Picnic Area. You can walk from the picnic area down to the river. By the river and the main road is the park's Boat Ramp and across the river from the boat ramp is the Primitive Camping Area, a scenic area on the Edisto River for use by organized groups.

After returning to the main road, don't miss driving, too, down to Cabin Lake that you can see on your map. This side road leads to the park's fourth lake and to the Canoe Take-Out Dock at the end of the 1.7-miles Water Trail on the Edisto River. A couple of park cabins sit across from the parking area, used by the park service, and you'll see the trail to the dock nearby. Cabin Lake is a pret-

ty lake and visitors can canoe, boat, and fish here or enjoy a picnic by the water at several picnic tables. An easy, soft-footed trail winds for a short distance along the lakeside with a rest bench where you can stop to enjoy looking across the water.

An interesting aspect of Aiken State Park is that there are several riding trails on the park's acreage, and there are 70 more miles of trails for horseback riding and hiking in nearby Hitchcock Woods in Aiken, a wooded park that covers 2,100 acres. Also, there are a large number of horse camps and equestrian resorts in the area with riding trails, horse boarding, camp sites, rental cottages, event barns and more. Many well-known equestrian events are held each year in the Aiken area,

and Aiken is often called a horse lovers paradise with nationally known polo matches, horse shows, fox hunts, a spring steeplechase, and the spring Carolina Cup horseracing event held here. Don't miss this great park and all the things to do and see in the Aiken area.

Barnwell State Park

Midlands - Barnwell County
Park Address: 223 State Park Road, Blackville, SC 29817
Park Size: 307 acres   Month Visited: August
Directions: From Interstate 20 south, take exit 18 or 20 to Aiken, take Hwy 78 to Blackville. Turn south on Hwy 3/Solomon Blatt Avenue in Blackville and follow three miles to park entrance and sign on right.

Park Description:

Barnwell is a small rural park developed around two small lakes that Toby Creek flows through before continuing on. The park is loved by locals and visitors for fishing and as a quiet spot for outdoor getaways and camping. It was one of many parks built by the Civilian Conservation Corps (CCC) in the 1930s Depression era, and many of the early structures still remain, like two pavilions, an old pumphouse and the park's pretty spillway.

On entering Barnwell's grounds, follow the road to the right past a pavilion to the park office. In the office building is a small store and gift shop, and if you arrive when it is closed, you will still find park maps, information, and area brochures by the office door. The park sponsors a Junior Ranger Program and the park rangers give fun and informative talks in summer and host a campfire program on Saturday nights.

On the lake not far from the park office are a meeting-community building for events and a recreation building near the swim beach. The community building, with its lovely lakeside views, a kitchen and a large meeting space that will accommodate over two-hundred people, is popular for gatherings, weddings, and reunions. The recreation building nearby, with spacious, separate bathhouses for both men and women, was one of our favorite spots in the park. It has a snack bar and pretty covered porches looking out toward the roped-off swimming area on the beach. There is also a swim raft in the deeper part of the lake, and near the recreation building are picnic tables and grills, a play area, and broad paved side-walks leading directly down to the lakeside. This is a really attractive spot for summer days and we enjoyed watching visitors playing in the swim area when we visited.

Further along the park road on the north side of the lake we discovered two pretty pavilions and five rental cabins at the end of the road. These cute octagonal cabins all have two bedrooms, kitchens, baths, and all the facilities of home, including pretty outdoor decks. For additional fun, there is a fine playground on this side of the lake, areas for volleyball and Frisbee, and easy access to the lake at every point. The road on the opposite side of the main lake leads to the park's campground and to another pavilion and a fishing pier that reaches out into the lake. Barnwell has twenty-five campsites on a loop road at the end of this second road, restrooms with showers, a dump station, and seventeen of the sites have electric and water for RVs. The campsites on the far end of the loop road look out onto the park's second lake, another favorite spot for fishing, with water lilies decorating the banks in many places.

There are two nice hiking or walking trails in Barnwell Park. One, the Dogwood Trail, loops around the main lake for 1.5 miles. It has access points at many spots along its way. We especially enjoyed the section of the trail that followed a long boardwalk around the spillway and on to the pretty fishing pier on the back of the lake. The long pier, renovated not long ago, looks across the lake to the community building and offers a good spot for fishing as well as fine views up and down the lake. The park's second trail, the 1.5-miles Fernhill Trail offers another easy walk on a well-maintained trail winding through the woods on a figure-eight loop. The trail is named for the abundance of ferns you will see on several portions of the trail. Although Barnwell is a small park, it is a charming and well-kept park to visit with pretty lakes and trails.

Congaree National Park

Midlands - Richland County
Park Address: 100 National Park Drive, Hopkins, SC 29061
Park Size: 26,276 acres   Month Visited: October
Directions: From Interstate 26 below Columbia, take Hwy I-77
across the Congaree River and turn south on Hwy 48/Bluff Road,
staying left as the road splits into Old Bluff Road. Follow Old
Bluff Road to National Park Drive and park entrance on right.

Park Description:

Of the seven National Park sites in South Carolina, Congaree is the state's only National Park. Protected under the Wilderness Act of 1964 and established as the Congaree Swamp National Monument in 1976, the land officially became a national park in 2003. The vast acreage is the largest tract of old growth bottomland hardwood forest in the United States. Although often called a swamp, it is actually a dynamic river floodplain with the waters from the Congaree and Wateree Rivers sweeping through it. The park has few of the amenities familiar to other parks and sites, but is instead a protected wilderness with 90 species of trees, including bald cypress and water tupelo, giant hardwoods and loblolly pines. Congaree also provides cover in its diverse ecosystem for an abundance of wildlife including deer, turkey, coyotes, wild pigs, bobcats, armadillos and otters. You may also see turtles, owls, birds, frogs, mammals, alligators, snakes and other reptiles, along with several species of fish. The park is a part of the internationally

recognized Biosphere Reserve of sites protected for exceptional biodiversity. Visiting it offers unique opportunities to see an old growth wilderness area and a chance to see synchronous fireflies between mid-May to mid-June.

The place to learn more about the park and to decide what parts of it to visit is at the Harry Hampton Visitor Center, a Nature Center and park office at the end of the main National Park Road. The center is named for reporter, editor, and outdoorsman Harry Hampton (1897-1980) who worked for *The State* newspaper in Columbia and began a campaign in the 1950s to save the Congaree River floodplain. Inside the Nature Center are wildlife and educational exhibits, park information and maps, and an 18-minute film to acquaint visitors with the natural wonder of the park. Outside the center is a "Mosquito Gauge" on the wall, with ratings from *1-All Clear* to *6-War Zone!*, a reminder to bring bug repellent to this park.

Congaree has 25 miles of hiking trails, from short, somewhat level easy walks to more moderate and difficult ones. Ten different trails are marked and described in the Congaree National Park Trail Guide. The most popular, loved by all ages—and often the only trail explored by most visitors—is the 2.6-miles Boardwalk Loop Trail which allows visitors to see a large portion of the floodplain wilderness on a boardwalk loop. The boardwalk begins through a wooden arch right behind the center to travel into an old growth bottomland and hardwood forest. In the early part of the trail an exit leads down to the 1.8-miles Bluff Trail and to a picnic area with a nice pavilion, and along the way rest benches and overlooks are built

into the boardwalk at different points. The trail then moves from a hardwood forest area into bottomland and marsh filled with tall loblolly pines, one over 150 feet tall, past giant water tupelo trees with swollen trunks, some eight feet thick, and past bald cypress trees with "knees" or stumps rising from their roots on the forest floor. These cypress trees can live for over 1000 years and the cypress, tulepo, and loblolly pine thrive in this floodplain environment. From the boardwalk you can also see fan-shaped dwarf palmetto and bamboo-looking switch cane growing thickly in the forest floor. At the back of the Boardwalk Trail is a large wooden overlook with rest benches on Weston Lake and a link to the 4.4-miles Weston Lake Loop Trail.

With limited time, we explored parts of several of the easier trails that most visitors might enjoy, a part of the Weston Lake Loop Trail, the Bluff Trail, and a piece of the 3.2-miles Sims Trail that also starts at the visitor center. On the south end of the park near the South Cedar Creek canoe launch area, we walked a short portion of the old 2.2-miles Bates Ferry Trail and the 12-mile Kingsnake Trail. Many of Congaree's trails are difficult for the average tourist and hikers should always check with the park office to learn if trails are open and in good

condition as flooding often washes out trails, bridges, and boardwalks.

For those who love to kayak and canoe in primitive backwater areas, Congaree offers over 25 miles of water trails. Visitors can bring boats or rent from nearby outfitters. Many of these outfitters lead tours through Congaree and rangers offer free tours in certain seasons of the year. The Cedar Creek Canoe Trail, 15 miles long, is one of the most popular trails. Boaters can launch at Bannister's Bridge or at the South Cedar Creek area. Boaters and hikers should be aware it is not uncommon to walk or paddle through large spider webs, to find downed trees or muddy, boggy areas hard to navigate, to encounter wildlife like venomous snakes and alligators, or to battle stinging insects, gnats, and mosquitoes.

For those wanting to spend more than a day at the park, Congaree has two campgrounds, both rustic with no running water or bathrooms. Trailers and RVs are not allowed in either campground, only tents. The Longleaf Campground, off the main park road before the Nature Center, is the largest, with ten sites situated about 100 yards from a gravel parking area. It has picnic tables, firepits and vault toilets in a wooded area. The second, Bluff Campground, more remote, has 6 sites and is situated off Carolina Sims Road, about a mile's hike from the Longleaf or visitor center parking area. Primitive Backcountry camping is also allowed but campers should check with the park office about appropriate sites and regulations. Keep in mind for your visit that unlike most SC parks, Congaree is a true wilderness park. A documentary titled *Roots in the River: The Story of Congaree Park* was produced in 2008, spotlighting the history of the park and including interviews with individuals instrumental in the park's unique creation.

Goodale State Park

Midlands - Kershaw County
Park Address: 650 Park Road, Camden, SC 29020
Park Size: 736 acres   Month Visited: October
Directions: From Interstate 20 take the Camden Exit and follow
Hwy 521/Broad Street into Camden. Turn east on DeKalb/Hwy 1
to right on Old Stagecoach Road for 2.4 miles, left on State Park
Road, and then follow to park sign and entrance on right.

Park Description:

Although Goodale is a small park, it is an interesting one with unique features to see and enjoy. Just outside of Camden and only forty minutes from Columbia, Goodale is easy to get to from the nearby interstate. As you drive into the park, the first building you will see is a nice Community Center on the left. With a kitchen, fireplace, and pretty screened porch, the center, which can accommodate up to sixty people, is a great spot for small gatherings, weddings, or reunions. The road continues on, soon with views of the lake, to the main parking area by a long, brick park office where you will find a visitor center, restrooms, and a place to get park information.

Across from the office is a small monument, flagpole, and park dedication. The park, conveyed by the county to the state in 1973, is named for a Camden forester and prominent political figure, N. R. Goodale, who spearheaded the effort to get the county to acquire the park in the 1950s.

Behind the park office is a recreation area with picnic tables, a wooden swing, children's playground, and pathways winding down to the 140-acres Grist Mill Lake, the centerpiece of the park. Fishing is excellent on the lake and anglers can bring boats with electric motors to launch at the park's boat ramp to catch bream, bass, and catfish. Even more popular is the three-mile Canoe Trail winding from the broader section of Grist Mill lake back into the more narrow finger of the lake that reaches into the cypress swamp environment. It takes about three hours to paddle the canoe trail in and out again and paddlers will see a diversity of wildlife on their route. Along the Canoe Trail are cypress trees, waterlilies and aquatic plants, wildflowers in the spring, birds like wood ducks, and you may spot one of the alligators or snakes who call this lake home.

To explore the park on foot, there is a 1.7-miles Big Pine Tree Nature Trail that begins near the ranger office and community building to wind back into a woodland to a loop turn and back again. Markers along the way identify trees, like cedars, tulip poplars, and dogwood, and there is also a Tree ID guide available at the park office or online that contains more information. The pathway crosses a small bridge along the way and the entire trail is an easy, well-maintained walk for all ages to enjoy.

Another quiet walking trail leads from the park office and recreation area to the dam and bridge at the back of the lake. Following over the bridge leads to a pleasant trail along the perimeter of Grist Mill Lake. This trail will take you closer to the cypress trees growing right out of the water and by patches of water lilies along the shoreline. Right after crossing the bridge, watch also for a tiered pathway dropping down behind the dam. You can take a short walk here along the creek to see fern, flowers in spring, and salamanders in the creek.

The park and surrounding area carry an old history dating back to the years before the Civil War era when the Adams gristmill was on the lake. For a sampling of the Civil War history of the area you can visit the nearby 107-acres Camden Revolutionary War site with a museum, battlefield, and the beautiful Kershaw-Cornwallis house and gardens.

Dreher Island State Park

Midlands - Newberry County
Park Address: 3677 State Park Road, Prosperity, SC 29127
Park Size: 348 acres   Month Visited: October
Directions: From Interstate 26 take Exit 91 to Chapin, turning right on Hwy 76 and then left onto St. Peters Church Rd/Hwy 29 for 4 miles. Take a left on Dreher Island Rd/Hwy 231 for 3 miles, then left onto State Park Road for 2 miles to park entrance.
Park Description:

Dreher Island State Park is an especially scenic park sprawling over not just one but three connected islands on beautiful Lake Murray. The small islands, each with fingers of land reaching out into the lake in different directions, are linked together by causeways and bridges. First known as Dreher Island Recreation Area in the 1970s, the property officially became a state park in 1990. Only thirty miles from Columbia, and yet tucked away in the countryside, this is a truly memorable place to visit.

After traveling over the long causeway into the park, you'll pass the fee station and a side road to one of the park's camping areas. Continue across another bridge to the Visitor Center and Park Store on the left. Inside you'll find park information, snacks, grocery items, ice, firewood, restrooms, a tackle shop, and the park's camping and villa registration center. On the porch are picnic tables, with more tables, two of the park's pavilions, and a playground nearby. Behind the store, a walkway leads downhill to a boat dock, boardwalk, and gas pump on Lake Murray. Continuing on Park Marina Drive, by the store, leads to the Dreher Island Marina. Behind the marina's office, snack shop and restrooms, a long pier reaches out into the lake to access 50 boat rental slips, each with water, electric, and sewer. This is a gorgeous spot with stunning views out over the lake.

Across from the visitor center and marina another side road swings down to one of Dreher's three boat docks, to a large pavilion, which is popular with tournament groups, and to more lake views and water access for boats, kayaks, and canoes. Lake Murray as a whole covers 50,000 acres and, with so much water, fishing is popular at this park with its twelve miles of shoreline. Several well-known Bass Tournaments are held at Dreher every year and fish most commonly caught on the lake are striped bass, largemouth and smallmouth bass, crappie, bream, perch and catfish. Dreher also offers a tackle loaner program with rods and reels, and SC fishing licenses, available at the park store.

Leaving Dreher's second island, you cross another bridge onto the park's third and largest island. As you swing right on Park Loop Road, take a right turn on White Oak Lane to find another picnic area, playground, pavilion, and the park's rustic

community building tucked on yet another peninsula. The community building can accommodate up to 75 people for group events. Next to the community center is the trail sign for the beginning of the Billy Dreher Nature Trail. The trail is named for Wm Henry "Billy" Dreher (1857-1938) who once lived on the land here. A scenic quarter-mile walk leads to the lake and back, traveling by the ruins of Dreher's old home.

After returning to the main road, pull over and stop at the second Park Office on the right. Behind it a long, lovely boardwalk travels back through the woods and out to fine lake views. Every side road at Dreher seems to offer yet another

delightful spot to see. A little further on, to the left, Red Maple Drive leads to more picnic pavilions and the park's ten cabins. These are small rustic 12 x 12 cabins for those who don't want to set up a tent. They have heat, air, lights and electric, bunks or beds to put your sleeping bag on, but no running water, bathrooms or kitchens. All the cabins share well-maintained restroom

facilities with hot showers and each looks out across the lake. These cute cabins have covered decks, picnic tables, outdoor grills and patios. For accommodations with more amenities, the next road on the right, Villa Lane, leads to five beautiful well-appointed rental villas with two or three bedrooms, kitchens, bathrooms, television, wifi and more. Winding pathways lead down from each villa to the lake and all share a private boat dock.

Near the cabins and villas is the start of the 2.1-miles Little Gap Trail which winds through the woods to end at a fine lake view. A side road near the beginning of the trail leads to a large primitive group camp area. And at the far end of the park a beautiful loop road winds through the larger of the park's two campground areas. In all, Dreher has over 100 campsites, for camping of all types, including travel trailers, large and small RVs, and tent campers, with water and electric, several comfort stations with restrooms and showers, and a dump station. Many sites are directly on the water for easy boating and fishing access. This park truly has something for everyone.

Sesquicentennial State Park

Midlands - Richland County
Park Address: 9564 Two Notch Road, Columbia, SC 29223
Park Size: 1419 acres   Month Visited: October
Directions: From Interstate 26 take Exit 107B and turn east on
Hwy 20. Follow to Exit 74/Hwy 1 (Two Notch Road). Travel north
three miles to park entrance on right.

Park Description:

       The Sesquicentennial Park, called "Sesqui" for short, offers a diversity of pleasures right on the outskirts of Columbia. After leaving a busy highway, the park entry road winds back through a pine and hardwood forest—soon leaving city noise behind. We stopped first at the big Retreat and Community Center on the left, attracted by the old log cabin there. The historic 1800s hand hewn cabin, brought to the park in the 1960s, is thought to be the oldest existing structure in the county, and a civic group and local family worked hard to save the cabin and move it to the park. Behind the parking lot beside the log cabin, a long conference center sprawls across a green rise. The facility can accommodate 60 for meetings and conferences and its dormitory can sleep 30. Next to the center is a fenced dog park with picnic tables and benches, a great place for dogs to romp off leash. At the end of the parking lot is the beginning of the Sesqui Mountain Bike Trail. The six-mile clay and dirt route travels on an easy trek through the park's woods to loop

and return. The wide, flat, and well-maintained trail is popular with visitors and locals alike, not only for biking but for hiking and walking dogs on leash.

Continuing on to the central part of Sesqui's grounds leads to the park office and a lovely, shady recreation area. Just before this area a right turn travels back into Sesqui's campground. The campground spreads around two interlinking loop roads with 84 campsites for trailers,

RVs, and tents, along with three comfort stations and a dump station. The camp road is shaded, smooth and sandy, a nice place for walking and biking and providing easy access for set-up. Off a winding side road the park also has a primitive camping area for up to 50 in a quiet location.

Within walking distance of both campgrounds is the park's broad, recreation area, looking out over beautiful 30-acre Sesqui Lake. The park office, located in a long gray building down a short paved path from the parking area, is the perfect spot to get park information, maps, and to enjoy the gift and souvenir shop. Next to the office is a Splash Pad, a unique aspect at Sesqui, popular with kids in the warm summer months. Scattered around the park office and Splash Pad area are wide grassy grounds, two children's playgrounds, and a multitude of pic-

nic tables and pretty pavilions looking out over the lake. A winding paved trail wanders through all, to the park's ballfield, and down to a long white boathouse by the lake. By the boathouse is a boat access area and a swim beach. Small non-motorized boats can be brought to the park and canoes, kayaks, paddleboards, and peddle boats can be rented at the boathouse. Fishing is enjoyed from boat or along the shorelines, and anglers catch bream, bass, crappie, and catfish.

A lovely paved trail wanders from the boathouse along the lakeside, a part of one of the park's hiking trails. The 2-miles Sandhills Hiking Trail circles the park's lake on a mostly paved trail through wetlands, along the lake, and on boardwalks through the marsh end of the park. The trail is well marked with white blazes, and a peaceful easy stroll through a shady woods. Dogs on leash are allowed on the trail and there are water points for dogs at two spots along the way. The entire trail takes less than an hour to walk and offers an opportunity to see two ponds, turtles, butterflies, lizards, mushrooms, a wide variety of birds, flowers, and other pleasures along the way.

Toward the back end of the lake, a side trail leads to another shorter park trail the half mile Jackson Creek Nature Trail. It trav-

els through a lowland area on boardwalks to wander through woodland to arrive finally at a spillway and pretty tiered waterfall display behind the dam. This lovely park, so near town, offers a multitude of pleasurable ways to spend a day out of doors.

While camping at the park or staying in the area there are many sites to visit around Columbia. At nearby Fort Jackson is a combat training museum and in Columbia is the South Carolina Military Museum for those interested in military history. On Marion Avenue is the Palmetto Falls Water Park, a nice play park for kids. Not far away is the Riverbanks Zoo and Botanical Garden with 2000 animals and over 350 species from around the world, plus beautiful gardens, an aquarium/reptile house, bird exhibit, petting zoo, splash pad, a train ride, a carousel, and zip lines. In nearby downtown Columbia are the historic Capitol building, the South Carolina State Museum, a children's museum, and a canal and riverfront park. Nearby, too, is local Saluda Shoals Park on the Lower Saluda River with walking trails, fishing, boating, biking , and more opportunities for outdoor pleasure. With Sesqui State park so near South Carolina's capital city, visitors won't lack for things to do and see.

Lake Wateree State Park

Midlands - Fairfield County
Park Address: 881 State Park Road, Winnsboro, SC 29180
Park Size: 238 acres   Month Visited: October
Directions: From Interstate 77 exit on either Hwy 97 through Great
Falls or Hwy 200 through Mitford and take Hwy 21 south to a left
turn on Wateree Road. Travel Wateree into the River Road at inter-
section and follow to State Park Rd and park entrance on left.

Park Description:

Although Lake Wateree State
Park didn't officially open until the 1980s,
the lake is one of the oldest lakes in South
Carolina, developed with the damming of
the Wateree River in 1919-1920. The lake
in its entirety, covering 13,864 acres and
touching three counties with 181 miles of
shoreline, was named for Wateree Native
Americans who once lived in the area.
Lake Wateree State Park, thirty miles from
Columbia and owned and managed by the
SC Department of Natural Resources, is
known for fishing, boating, and the boun-
tiful wildlife along its shoreline. Having
spent a happy summer vacation at a lakeside home nearby, we'd already developed
an appreciation and love for Lake Wateree
even before visiting the park.

To make our visit even more fun,
we arrived not long before Halloween
when Lake Wateree rangers and workers decorate the park for its annual Creepy
Campout Halloween Event. The park entry sign was covered with spider webs,

a giant spider hung on the front of the fee station, and a friendly ghost grinned at us by the roadside as we entered the park, letting us know right away we were in for some extra Halloween smiles on our Wateree visit. More Halloween fun greeted us as we crossed the bridge over Taylor Creek into the main park area and spotted a skeleton casting his line off the bridge and two more skeletons fishing from a boat in the lake below.

Entering the park we followed the signs to Wateree's visitor center, office, and tackle shop. Inside the office you can pick up maps, information, gift items, souvenirs, snacks, ice, firewood, and groceries, especially helpful to campers and park visitors as the closest grocery stores are about twenty minutes away in Mitford or Great Falls. Behind the visitor center we caught our first full glimpse across the broad expanse of Lake Wateree. After leaving the park office a nice walk took us through shaded picnic areas with benches alongside the lake to Wateree's boat launch, fishing pier, dock and fuel station. We also passed a pretty playground along the way with great climbing structures, slides, and a bench for mom or dad. In addition, Wateree has a swim area at the beach, rods and reels for rent at the park office, and winding roads throughout the park for biking.

The area alongside the lake was busy with boaters and anglers on the warm October day we visited. This state park is a fine place for boating, either in kayaks, canoes, or motorboats, and fishing is excellent on the lake. Many area fishing tournaments are held at Wateree and fish caught include largemouth bass, stripers, white bass, crappie, catfish, white perch, shellcrackers, and bream. We spotted many boats out on the water, even on our weekday visit, as well as anglers along the shore enjoying the mild day.

North of the park office and marina area a loop road leads through a picturesque campground, with 23 sites directly on the waterfront. The park has 100 paved

campsites with picnic tables and grills for trailers, RVs, and tents. All have electric and water hookup and 28 also have sewer, and the campground has a dump station and two comfort stations with hot showers. We loved driving through this beautiful campground, especially since many decorations for the upcoming weekend Halloween event were already up. We laughed over big Halloween balloons, carved pumpkins of

all kinds, a mock graveyard, ghosts swinging from the trees, skeletons camping out by their tents and campfire, and other innovative displays all around the camp area. Over the Halloween weekend during the Creepy Campground Halloween Event prizes are given for the best campsite decorations, best golf cart decorations, and best costumes. The park hosts a Halloween scavenger hunt, a pumpkin carving contest, and trick or treating hours on Halloween from 6:30 to 9:00. A nearby church has a fall festival at the same time and they offer a haunted hayride through the park and give out candy, as well. As you can imagine, campsites fill up quickly in the park at this time of year.

Wateree has one nature trail, a little over two miles in length, that starts near the main parking lot. The Desportes Nature Trail, named for the Desportes Island the main park sits on, is wide, flat and offers an easy hike for all ages. We walked the left loop down to the lake, passing wetlands along the left, a rest bench, and ending with a fine view across the lake. There's a nice quiet fishing spot at the trail's end, too. Another loop piece of the trail leads out to the right to a peninsula on Duchman or Dutchman's Creek.

Across the creek from this spot on the west side of the park, the River Road leads to a bridge crossing over the creek. Dutchman's Creek Marina sits across from the park boundary before the bridge begins and has a small store and a restaurant, popular with area campers and visitors. A second walking trail follows across the long bridge over Dutchman's Creek, offering great lake views and a good spot for bridge fishing.

Edisto Beach

LOWCOUNTRY SOUTH CAROLINA STATE PARK INDEX

LOWCOUNTRY
South Carolina
PARKS

Charles Towne Landing

Hunting Island

Givhans Ferry

Santee

Edisto Beach State Park

Lowcountry - Charleston County
Park Address: 8377 State Cabin Rd, Edisto Island, SC 29438
Park Size: 1255 acres   Month Visited: August
Directions: From I-26, take Mark Clark Expressway 526 before
Charleston to Hwy 17; turn south on US Hwy 174; turn right at
Environmental Learning Center sign and follow to visitor center.

Park Description:

     Edisto Beach State Park has a large acreage spanning across two sides
of Hwy 174, including both scenic maritime forest and saltmarsh land plus beach
front property on the Atlantic Ocean. The park was built by the CCC (Civilian
Conservation Corps) in the 1930s. Edisto State Park sits on one of the more remote sea islands along the Atlantic coast, the area less commercial than similar
resort islands. The park is about an hour from either Charleston to the north or
Beaufort to the south, nice for side trip excursions.

     We started our exploration of the park by turning onto Palmetto Road at
the Environmental Learning Center park sign and following the road to the park
entrance on the left and on to the Learning Center and park office. This is a great
place to get maps and directions to all areas of the park, to ask questions, and
to explore the center. Exhibits there feature interactive displays about the coast
and park area. The center offers interpretive programs and we enjoyed all the
interesting exhibits about Edisto's coastal history, birds, alligators, turtles, and

other wildlife. The building is beautiful, too, with porches on back with rockers and woodland views. Branching out from the back of the center are several of the park's hiking trails. The Edisto park has seven trails and there is a nice YouTube about them on the park's website. All trails are suitable for hiking and biking and are flat, sandy, and easy to walk. On most days, however, it's wise to spritz with bug spray before heading out on these coastal trails.

The Bache Monument Trail leads for 0.2-miles from the environmental center to a historic granite marker. Along the trail are kiosks explaining the importance of the survey marker the trail leads to. The monument is the oldest marker still intact as a part of Alexander Bache's early measurements of the U.S. Coast in 1850. On the way back, we took a side trail to walk the long boardwalk out to the Education Dock on Big Bay Creek. The scenes up and down the creek were beautiful and the walk an easy one.

Returning to the center we headed over to hike the 0.4-miles Big Bay Trail to the Spanish Mount next. This trail winds through the woods to end at a kiosk explaining the mounds of Indian shells you can see piled by the creek

below. Walking down the trail to see the mounds we looked over to spot two kayakers on the creek below us. This area is a wonderful one for kayaking, canoeing, and fishing, and there is a wide boat ramp and parking area near the center for access to the creek. There are no boat rentals at the state park but at Edisto Beach nearby several water sports businesses rent canoes and kayaks and offer boat tours around the marshes and island area. For a longer hike, the Big Bay Trail connects to the Spanish Mount Trail, but we turned to head back to check out the other park areas next.

From the visitor center, we drove back up Palmetto Road, turned right on Hwy 174 and drove to the next park section leading back to Live Oak Campground and the park's cabins. There is a cabin and camper check-in point not far from the highway's entrance, and the campground has sites for both RV and tent campers. Further down the road are a cluster of cabins to rent looking out over Scott Creek and the salt marsh. Several trails wind out from the Live Oak Campground. We enjoyed hiking the 0.4-miles Big Bay Trail that led over a long boardwalk across the salt marsh. Campers also can enjoy using the Edisto Bike Trail, leading for 0.4-miles along the paved causeway directly to the beach from the campground.

Heading to the beach was our next stop in this park. The park's beach entrance is just across from the island supermarket and gas station on Hwy 174. The road leads back into Edisto Beach State Park's long stretch of land directly along the Atlantic Ocean. The park has a lovely one-and-a-half mile stretch of beautiful private beachfront property with eight beach access points for visitors and campers. There is also a gracious, tree-shaded picnic area near the main parking area beside the big park office and store. Inside campers

can pick up basic supplies and tourists can find souvenirs, beach gear, drinks, snacks, and park information. The park's two pavilions are not far from the office and some nice trails wind back through the wooded area leading to the camping areas beyond. Driving back down the winding road into the campground, it is easy to see why these sites are so sought after by visitors. There is even another small store toward the far back end of the campground loop road and campers here have access to a multitude of quiet spots on the beach and many have views of the salt marsh and Scott Creek running behind the campground area. Altogether the park has 120 camp sites, most with electric and water, plus additional tent site areas.

This beach end of the park is within easy biking and walking distance to stores, shops, and local restaurants at Edisto Beach. Campers and visitors to the park can enjoy touring the island, riding its bike trails, and driving around to the marina and waterside park on Big Bay Creek. On the highway coming in to the park are a post office, shops, stores, a bookstore, more restaurants, and other

attractions to enjoy including historic buildings and churches, a Serpentarium, and the Edisto Museum. An additional treat at Edisto is the 4,600-acres Botany Bay Plantation Wildlife Management Area open to the public to tour. It contains ruins of plantation buildings, wildlife and plants, trails, and the old "Boneyard Beach" with an abundance of shells. Put this park and this scenic island on your "places to visit" list.

Hunting Island State Park

Lowcountry - Colleton County
Park Address: 2555 Sea Island Pkwy, Hunting Island, SC 29920
Park Size: 5000 acres   Month Visited: August
Directions: From I-95 south, take Beaufort exit Hwy 17/21,
continuing on Hwy 21 (Sea Island Pkwy) thru Ladies Island and
St. Helena Island and over Johnson Creek on the Harbor River
Bridge to Hunting Island and state park sign.

Park Description:

The place to begin exploring Hunting Island State Park is near the middle of the park at the visitor center. Follow the long forested entry road to the third turn on the left. After passing through the Fee Station, the road winds its way back to the center, tucked in a scenic marshy spot with a long boardwalk leading to the center's entrance. The green marsh covering the pond around the center is called "duckweed" and is a floating plant alive with creatures that thrive above and below its surface, including alligators—if you can spot one. A fountain burbles in the middle of this marshy wilderness and there is a covered back porch with rocking chairs at the center's entrance. Inside the newly renovated visitor center are many interactive exhibits to enjoy. Touch screen displays feature videos telling about the lighthouse, the island's ecology, sea turtles, and the Civilian Conservation Corps (CCC) who built the park in the 1930s. At the center you can get brochures and information about what to see and do in the park and pick up a map to help you find your way around more easily.

From the visitor center we headed to the Hunting Island Lighthouse, the park's centerpiece attraction. The lighthouse was originally built in 1857, rebuilt after the Civil War, and moved inland in 1889 when the encroaching sea threatened it. In the

1930s Franklin D. Roosevelt determined Hunting Island a good site for development of a state park, and in 1941 the park opened. The lighthouse, whose light once projected nearly 20 miles out to sea, was decommissioned in 1933 but still has a functional light that can be seen for about five miles. The beautiful 136-foot lighthouse is the only lighthouse in South Carolina that allows visitors to

climb its 167 stairs to the high observation deck for stunning panoramic views. At the lighthouse station, around the lighthouse, are several historic buildings to explore and a lighthouse keeper to answer any questions you might have. Across from the lighthouse is the Lighthouse Gift Shop, a good place to pick up gifts, postcards, and to buy snacks and drinks you can eat outside at one of the picnic tables under the trees or at the nearby pavilion. Just beyond the lighthouse area, too, is a beautiful stretch of beach for fun by the ocean.

Hunting Island State Park runs for five miles along the Atlantic Ocean with beaches to enjoy at the North Beach Area and midway along the island at the South Beach

area. At both beach areas there are picnic tables, pavilions, and restrooms. The once popular beach area, at the park's southern end, and the beloved, historic cabins built by the CCC were destroyed by Hurricane Matthew, 2016, and Hurricane Irma, 2017. You can still walk to this beach area but the old Cabin Road, once stretching to the southern end of the island, was washed out and is now closed to cars. The one remaining park rental cabin is just outside the lighthouse station grounds called the Lighthouse Cabin.

Hunting Island State Park, which covers 5000 acres of land, lagoons, and salt marshes has twelve trails scattered around its grounds you can walk or bike. One begins near the South Beach Pavilion and parking lot, the 1.0-mile Lagoon Trail. It winds along the side of the park's lagoon, with pretty views along the way, to the southern end of the park. On its route, this trail links via several connector trails to the long 2-mile Maritime Forest Trail and to the 1.9-miles Diamondback Rattlesnake Trail for a longer hike or biking trip. For all the park trails into the maritime forest or along the lagoons or marshes, we'd advise bug spray, as the mosquitoes and insects are sometimes pesky.

Leaving the South Beach pavilion area, we drove back toward the park entrance to check out the campground area. The park has over one hundred standard campsites and a rustic tent camping area, with restrooms, a dump station, playground, and a nice park store, all in a scenic area with easy access to the beach. From the campground, we drove south on the main road again, which skirts along the salt marsh and Johnson Creek. We stopped at the Wildlife Viewing Area to look out over the salt marshes, read the info at the kiosk near the covered viewing deck and then walked out over the long board-walk to enjoy the views. A short distance down the road we stopped again to walk out on another long, beautiful boardwalk at the 0.25-miles Marsh Boardwalk Trail. This boardwalk leads over the salt marsh to a small island and then on across more marshland to an inlet and a second viewing deck, which is a great spot for bird watching and viewing the sunset.

At the end of the road a right turn leads down to the park's boat ramp and a left turn to the park's Nature Center, which you should definitely plan to visit. The Nature Center sits on stilts beside Fripp Island Inlet at the end of the island. Inside are wonderful wildlife exhibits, live sea animals, and a nice gift shop. Additionally, a park naturalist offers free public programs most days about the barrier island and its wildlife. Behind the center a 120-foot fishing pier stretches into Fripp Inlet with wonderful views across the water and marshlands. We saw egrets and other water birds here and enjoyed watching kayaks, boats, and people fishing off the pier.

A short distance from the Nature Center we walked another of the park's trails, the Nature Center Scenic Trail. It led for just over a half mile back through the maritime forest on an easy sandy pathway to travel to a pedestrian bridge. The bridge leads across to the new island created when a breach formed between the lagoon and ocean. Although sometimes the tide or a storm intrudes on part of the island, there is an 0.5-miles loop path, the Little Hunting Island Loop Trail, you can walk to explore the area. On the island you'll find petrified trees, driftwood, and lovely views. A second Breach Trail also leads to the area where the breach between the ocean and the lagoon formed. You'll find many interesting things to see and do in this beautiful seaside state park.

Rivers Bridge State Park

Lowcountry - Bamberg County
Park Address: 225 State Park Road, Ehrhardt, SC 29081
Park Size: 390 acres   Month Visited: August
Directions: From I-95 south, take Walterboro exit 57 at Hwy 64.
Travel west on Hwy 64/Bells Hwy, turning left onto Hwy 641
(Confederate Hwy) at the road split. Follow Hwy 641 crossing 601
intersection leading to Ehrhardt, and continue on to park sign and
south entrance on State Rd S-5-8.

Park Description:

Rivers Bridge State Park and Historic Site is a small park commemorating the site of the Confederacy's last stand against Union General William Sherman's army as they advanced across the South near the end of the Civil War. Within the park are historic battlefield trails and old roadways of historic significance, a preserved battlefield site, memorial grounds, four historic cemeteries, monuments, and a small museum dedicated to the casualties of the battle held there. The park is mainly a historic site and it has few other amenities except for picnic areas, shelters, and a rental community building.

Begin your visit to the park at the Visitor Center where you can pick up a map and information to help you find your way around to the different sites in the park. Here you will learn that a memorial association eventually obtained the battlefield acreage and in 1945 turned the property over to South Carolina for a state park and state historic site.

Close to the visitor center is a wide trail lined with split-railed fencing leading to the Memorial Grounds where the Confederate dead are interred. At the Memorial Grounds you will find the Rivers Bridge Relic Room, Civil War monuments, flags, a Confederate Cemetery, World War II monuments and a cemetery dedicated to their remembrance. Kiosks and signs around the property help to explain the historical monuments you are viewing.

From the Memorial Grounds you will see a trail sign linking to the 1.0-mile Historic Causeway Road that connects the Memorial Grounds to the preserved Rivers Bridge Battlefield or you can drive down the road to the battlefield. On the 0.8-miles Battlefield Trail you will find interpretive panels that explain the historic battle of 1865 and see the earthworks where the Confed-

erates made their heroic trench warfare battle stand. Guided tours are given by park rangers every Saturday, and reenactments of the battle are often staged in February by various private organizations.

History Note:

By 1864 in the Civil War (1861-1865), with Grant in command of Union forces and Sherman moving in to take Atlanta, the tide of the war was turning in favor of the North, and Sherman and his army began their devastating "March to the Sea." On this route the Battle of Rivers Bridge was fought on February 2nd and 3rd in 1865 in a valiant effort by the South to stop the path of Sherman's March. General Sherman had led his army into South Carolina in January and then moved his unit of over five thousand Union soldiers to attempt to take Rivers Bridge and cross the Salkehatchie River. Amazingly with only twelve hundred Confederate soldiers General Layfayette McLaws led Colonel Harrison's brigade division in a strong defense, holding off Sherman's men for almost two days until additional Union reinforcements arrived. The battle cost both armies about one hundred casualties each. The win for Sherman allowed his army to move forward in its victory march through the South. The war ended not many months later when Lee surrendered to Grant at Appomattox Courthouse, Virginia, on April 9th, 1865.

143

Lake Warren State Park

Lowcountry - Hampton County
Park Address: 1079 Lake Warren Road, Hampton, SC 29924
Park Size: 440 acres   Month Visited: August
Directions: From I-95 south, take Yemmassee exit onto Hwy 68 west. Follow Hwy 68/Yemmassee Hwy to Varnville. Turn left on Hwy 601/Savannah Hwy and then right on Lake Warren Road and follow to park sign.

Park Description:

We arrived at Lake Warren State Park in the late afternoon after a day of rain to find everything especially green and lush in this small state park. Although the park has a large acreage around Lake George Warren, only an approximately 90-acre tract on both sides of the lake has been developed for recreation access. Convenient to get to, Lake Warren State Park is only about nine minutes from nearby Hampton, a charming city with historic buildings from the 1800s, lodging, restaurants, and shops.

Even though Lake Warren State Park is small it is well laid out and offers something for everyone to enjoy—fishing, boating, hiking trails, picnic areas, a playground, and idyllic views out across the 200-acres lake. On the left after entering the park you'll find a small office and restrooms beside a picnic area and pavilion. Behind the picnic area, look for the 1.25-miles Interpretive Trail. The first section is also a Fitness Trail with exercise stations and then the pathway loops back through the woods before returning to its beginning. We hiked left toward the park entrance, which led in about a quarter of a mile to the Park Pond. You'll find an observation deck and overlook here that looks out over this pretty two-acre pond. You might also spot water birds on this pond like herons, egrets, or other wading shorebirds. Warren State Park is known for its variety of birds from shorebirds to eagles, owls, hawks, kites, and songbirds.

It is also known for alligators, which you might spot at the pond or in the lake.

Across the road from the park office are two more pavilions and a children's playground. A trail leads from the playground down to a floating dock on the lake and a scenic fishing pier that ends in a long covered observation site. Be sure to walk out to the end of this long fishing pier to enjoy fine views of Lake Warren. Across the lake you will spot the park's boat ramp, where anglers can launch their boats into the water. The park also rents small jon boats to visitors to enjoy a day on the water. Lake Warren is a shallow lake, only about 4-5 feet deep except around its two creek beds, which can reach 20 feet in depth. Anglers catch crappie, large-mouth bass, sunfish, and catfish on the lake and some call the lake an anglers' paradise.

Behind the playground is a second park trail, the short 0.3-miles Yemassee Nature Trail. It winds in an easy loop walk through the woods and to the lake. Both the park trails are well-maintained and scenic to walk on. There is no campground with amenities for RVs and tent camping at Lake Warren State Park, but there is a primitive Group Camp area behind the park office. If no groups are renting the site individuals can camp there and use the park's public restrooms not far away.

At the end of the main park road, after passing the ranger's residence, you will come to a beautiful Community Building, which can be rented for events. The meeting space can accommodate up to 80 people and the building has a kitchen, pretty porches, and scenic views of the lake. A trail from the parking area at the Community Building leads down to another fishing pier on Lake Warren. For a fun-filled day on a beautiful lake, this is an appealing park to visit.

Charles Towne Landing State Park

Lowcountry - Charleston County
Park Address: 1500 Old Towne Rd, Charleston, SC 29407
Park Size: 644 acres   Month Visited: August
Directions: From I-26 coming in to Charleston, take exit 216A onto Hwy 7 South. Travel Hwy 7, bearing left at split into Old Towne Road to park entrance and sign on left. Follow Old Towne Plantation Road through the park to the main parking lot.

Park Description:

      This fabulous state park proved to be one of our favorites in the South Carolina Lowcountry, so be sure to put it on your "must visit" list. Nestled in West Ashley near downtown Charleston, it's a pleasant surprise to simply drive into this quiet and beautiful park, where you soon forget about the busy traffic and streets you passed through. Charles Towne is a "walking and biking park," so come prepared to walk or bike for two miles on the well maintained, paved trails that lattice the grounds. Bikers can bring their own bikes or rent them, and for the less adventurous there is a park shuttle that loops through the park about every 20 minutes.

      A tall historic marker beside the parking lot reminds you that Charles Towne, established in 1670, was the first permanent English settlement in what is now South Carolina. Inside the visitor center you can tour the fine Exhibit

Hall and learn more about the history of Charleston and this remarkable park. While at the visitor center, be sure to look through the gift shop and pick up a map to help you find your way around the park. Beside the visitor center is a large shady picnic area, one of several in the park, and you will also spot behind the parking lot the Founders Hall, a spacious facility with large and small event

rooms that can be rented for meetings and gatherings. In addition, the historic Antebellum Legare-Waring House on the Charles Towne property is available for event rentals and is especially popular for weddings.

Studying our colorful map and following the park signs, we first walked to visit the Animal Forest. This is a 22-acre zoo with animals in their natural habitats. As you walk through the shady pathways and across natural bridges you will see a wide variety of animals and birds, such as bear, deer, bison, elk, eagles, and pelicans. Informative signs tell about the wildlife you are seeing and, along the pathway and within the Animal Forest, you'll also find rest benches, an outdoor classroom building, and restrooms.

As we returned to the main path, we passed the Native American wooden statue "Landing Brave," carved by sculptor Peter Toth, followed the signs to a small African American Cemetery and then walked on past another picnic area to a second Native American statue, Casique, a chief of the Kiawah, beside a pond. Our pathway next led us to a circular area around the Harry-Lucas ruins, an archeological site, and then on to the park's Original Settlement area with replicas of cabins, buildings, gardens, palisade walls, and even a stocks and pillory, that might have existed in the early years of Charles Towne. The crop garden is interesting with markers to identify the plants, along with fun information and facts. Inside the Common House you can see old furnishings, clothing, and guns of the period.

Moving on led us to the southernmost section of the park, looking out across the Ashley River. A little further on we found a row of 17th Century cannons, which would have protected the old fort once at Charles Towne Landing. These are working cannons and during park demonstrations or reenactment events, the cannons are still fired. As the walkway looped around by the water, we spotted the Adventurer ship with its tall masts, tied to a small dock, a reproduction of a fine 17th century coastal cargo vessel that would have carried passengers, supplies or livestock. You can climb aboard the ship to check it out up close, imagining what it might have been like to travel down the river and out onto the sea in an old sailing ship.

After passing the Adventurer, the ongoing pathway wandered through a salt marsh, winding across pretty boardwalks under old oaks draped in Spanish moss. Following a curve in the path, we next found ourselves looking down an Avenue

of Oakes, just like in *Gone With the Wind*, to the Antebellum plantation home that once belonged to Dr. Joseph Waring and his wife Ferdinanda. A plaque with a portrait tells you of Ferdinanda's devotion to this home she inherited and how she dedicated her latter life to restoring the home and grounds, and creating extensive gardens, scenic lagoons and fountains, and the avenue of oaks.

A side trail near the house weaves its way through Mrs. Waring's Gardens. In the spring the gardens are a glory with camellias of all colors, magnolias, azaleas, wisteria, and many other flowering trees and shrubs. Wandering through Ferdinanda's garden also takes you by a lake with a lovely fountain, to a shady garden alcove with benches, and to Christopher's Garden, a memorial for a little 10-year old boy. As the walkway around the park draws to an end, it winds past more picnic tables and a bird viewing area before you come again to the visitor center and exhibit hall… making you sad to see your visit draw to a close.

149

Reconstruction Era National Historic Park

Lowcountry - Beaufort County
Park Address: 706 Craven Street, Beaufort, SC 29902
Park Size: 65 acres   Month Visited: August
Directions: From I-95 south, take Beaufort exit, Hwy 17/21. Follow Hwy 21 into downtown Beaufort, and before Woods Memorial Bridge, turn right onto Cravens Street. Follow one block to park office across from The Arsenal.

Park Description:

The Reconstruction Era National Historic Park is a new SC park recognizing historic buildings and places important to the Reconstruction Era that followed the American Civil War. A campaign to establish the park began nearly twenty years ago. A proposal for the designation of these historic sites was introduced in President Clinton's administration, established in Obama's administration in 2017, and turned into a national historic park under the National Park Service as a part of a public lands bill signed by President Trump in March 2019. This bill re-designated the four existing sites and added plans for expansion of the park to include more Reconstruction sites in the future. The primary reason Beaufort was chosen for this memorial park is that it was one of the first places in the U.S. where freed slaves voted, bought property, created churches, and began schools and businesses.

Unlike many self-contained parks in a singular acreage, this park is spread out to encompass four main sites at this time. The place to begin is in downtown Beaufort at the park's Visitor Center located in the old Beaufort firehouse across from the historic Arsenal on Craven Street. There is no free parking area here, but you will find metered street parking on Craven and nearby streets. Inside the visitor center you will find a small museum, and you can talk to park rangers, pick up information, and attain a map to help you locate each section of the park.

At the second site, the Camp Saxton site on the Beaufort River, also sometimes called

Emancipation Grove, over 3000 freed slaves gathered to hear the Emancipation Proclamation read aloud in 1863. The old camp and ruins of former Fort Frederick in Port Royal lie south of Beaufort on the campus of the Beaufort Naval Hospital. This area will be developed for tourist visitation later, but was closed to the public at our visit.

The third and fourth sites in the Restoration Park are in the Penn Center area on St. Helena Island. After crossing the bridge from downtown Beaufort, travel on Hwy 21, the Sea Island Parkway, for seven miles to Martin Luther King Jr. Drive and the Penn Center sign. Turn right and drive down the road for a short distance to the park's third site on your left, an old historic church called The Brick Church. Built by black slaves in 1855, it later became their place of worship following the Civil War. An early school was established here and many civil rights leaders, including Dr. Martin Luther King, visited and spoke here. Walk around the church grounds and the cemetery behind it before driving on down the street to the final site in the park in the Penn Center.

The Penn Center is an African-American cultural and educational center and many of its buildings hold historic significance. After turning right into the center by the flags, follow the road around to the Penn Center Welcome Center. There you can learn more about this site's rich history, pick up helpful information, and then walk around to see many of the old buildings. At this time only Darrah Hall is officially designated as a part of the Reconstruction Era Park. You can walk to see this building, a simple white house, that is the oldest structure on the campus and was also one of the first schools in the South for freed slaves. You will learn a lot about a compelling slice of past U.S. history while exploring the different parts of this historic park.

Colonial Dorchester State Historic Park

Lowcountry - Dorchester County
Park Address: 300 State Park Rd, Summerville, SC 29902
Park Size: 325 acres   Month Visited: August
Directions: From I-26 south, take the Ladson Exit onto State Rd
S-8-62. Turn right at the Hwy 78 intersection onto Ladson Road
and follow to intersection of Hwy 642/Dorchester Road. Turn
right on Dorchester to the park entrance and sign on left.

Park Description:

      This small, scenic historic park, on the National Register of Historic
Places, gives visitors a look into the Lowcountry's Colonial past. The park sits
on the site where an early trading town flourished from 1697 through the Revolutionary War. The town began in 1690 when a group of Congregationalist settlers
came from Dorchester, Massachusetts. They soon established a flourishing town
with a church, businesses, a school, and eventually over forty homes. In 1719 the
settlers built St. George's Anglican Church for worship, later adding a tall brick
bell tower in 1751. For fortification and protection, they constructed a powder
magazine and a tabby fort of oyster shells and concrete on the Ashley River in
1757. The remains of the old Fort Dorchester, the Anglican brick church tower,
and an old cemetery can still be seen on the park grounds. In the park's small
museum you can see a model of what the town once looked like.

      On our visit to the park, we explored the fort and read the interpre-

tive kiosks and signs telling bits of history, walked some quiet trails around the park and down an old trade road to the Ashley River. The settlers used the river for trade and transportation and at low tide you can spot the remains of an old shipping dock. Near the fort we found a picnic area and restrooms and crossing the road led us to the pretty old church tower. Beside the tower, in the old cemetery, we studied graves dating back to the 1700s.

The oldest was for John Joor, a planter and merchant, who died in 1772. Other early graves were for James Postell and Charles Ladson, and there were many generations of Hutchinson graves enclosed in a brick wall. Near the cemetery was an archeological dig site, where the park is working to learn more of Dorchester's past.

By the time of the Revolutionary War (1775-1783), Dorchester had grown into a thriving town. During the war years the town and fort became a strategic point and many battles between the Patriots and the British were held here. Prominent figures enter into the town's history in this time and in 1775, in the early years of the Revolutionary War, Francis Marion, the Swamp Fox, commanded the garrison at Fort Dorchester. After the Revolutionary War ended, the town of Dorchester began to decline, perhaps due to destruction of property and disheartenment. The reasons are uncertain, but by 1788 the town of Dorchester was abandoned and its history nearly forgotten over the years. The surrounding forest and later a community park protected the site as the years passed, and thankfully in the mid 1900s, interest in the old town revived. In the 1960s land was acquired for a historic park and site and in 1969 the site was donated to the State Park Service. Today it's a quiet park for picnics, walks, and learning about South Carolina's history.

Fort Sumter
National Monument and Visitor Education Center

Lowcountry - Charleston County
Park Address: 340 Concord Street, Charleston, SC 29401
Park Size: 2.4 acres   Month Visited: August
Directions: Follow Interstate 26 south into downtown Charleston.
Exit onto Rutledge Avenue. Turn left on Calhoun. Continue on
Calhoun to parking garage near Liberty Square.

Park Description:

     Fort Sumter, a sea fort on the National Register of Historic Places, is about one mile out in the harbor from downtown Charleston, South Carolina. The fort was built after the War of 1812 to protect the Southern coast and named after General Thomas Sumter, a Revolutionary War hero. The fort is best known, however, as the site where the American Civil War began in 1861.

     The place to begin learning about Fort Sumter is at the Visitor Education Center in downtown Charleston at Liberty Square. If desired, visitors can also take a ferry from the Visitor Center, for a fee at regularly scheduled times, to tour Fort Sumter and explore the old fort up close. All ferries to the fort are operated by Fort Sumter Tours and the trip to the fort, a one-hour tour of the fort conducted by park rangers, and the trip back takes about two-and-a-half hours.

     At this park visit, we chose to only tour the wonderful Visitor

Education Center at Liberty Square. Inside the center is an excellent museum with interpretive and visual exhibits about Fort Sumter's history and the chain of events leading up to the Civil War. We enjoyed studying and reading all the information in the exhibits, seeing pictures of leaders, generals, and others who were a part of this early period of U.S. history, and

studying artifacts, like cotton bales, coins, an old flag, and more. We walked out on the dock behind the center to look out to sea to where the fort sat at a distance and also toured the ferry waiting area below the building. There we enjoyed a free, informative film about Fort Sumter, including the history of the fort and visuals of the rangers conducting tours around the fort's ruins, cannons, gun emplacements and more. If you don't have time to take the boat to the fort, look for this film for a lovely mini-visit to this historic landmark.

History Note:

After decades of disagreements over states rights and, especially, the underlying issue of slavery, a chain reaction of political events between 1860 and 1861 finally exploded into a Civil War. When Abraham Lincoln was elected to the office of President of the United States in March 1861, his election served as a catalyst to war for the South because of Lincoln's oppositional views to slavery and his belief that slavery was morally wrong. Between 1860 to1861,

eleven states in the Lower and Upper South seceded, or severed their ties with the Union. Although the South claimed the right to secede, the Government disputed that right and insisted the secession an act of rebellion that would initiate disunity and anarchy. The actual event that triggered the beginning of the Civil War was when in direct defiance of the government's ruling, Confederate leaders ordered an attack on the federal garrison at Fort Sumter on April 12, 1861, with the Union responding with defense.

Givhans Ferry State Park

Lowcountry - Colleton County
Park Address: 746 Givhans Ferry Rd, Ridgeville, SC 29472
Park Size: 988 acres   Month Visited: August
Directions: From Interstate 26 south take Ridgeville Exit onto
Hwy 27 south. Follow thru Ridgeville to Hwy 61. Turn north on
Hwy 61 and follow to County Rd 3-18-30. Turn left and travel to
park sign and Givhans Ferry Road.

Park Description:

Givhans Ferry State Park was one of the earlier sixteen SC state parks built by the Civilian Conservation Corps (CCC) and it officially opened in 1937. The park has a nice campground and cabins and is only 35 miles from nearby Charleston and approximately an hour to area beaches. The park was named for Thomas Phillip Givhan, who operated the Givhans Ferry on the Edisto River in the 1700s. Givhan was a well-to-do business-man, a supporter of the Revolution, a re-spected citizen, a road commissioner, and a devout Christian. Old records show that circuit rider Rev. Francis Asbury stayed at the Givhans' large home on the bluff above the Edisto River during many visits to the Lowcountry area.

After entering the park and pass-ing the Welcome Station, follow the road to the right to the park office in the Riverfront Hall. If you miss the office's hours, you'll find a map and brochures outside the door. The Riverfront Hall is a beautiful meeting facility that can ac-

commodate up to 100 people, with a kitchen and a huge back porch overlooking the Edisto River. A big wooden swing sits in a shady spot in front of the park office, and beyond it is a path leading to a side road down to the river and a fine sandy swim beach.

Across the street from the office you will spot a large shady park with swings, play equipment, and picnic tables. At the back of the playground is one of the entrances to the 1.5-miles (3 miles Round-Trip) River Bluff Nature Trail. The hike is a well-maintained pretty woods trail with benches along the way, a footbridge over a creek and views of the river from a bluff. The trail is an in-and-out one for both hiking and biking, but can be made into a 2-mile loop by returning on the road at the trail's end back to the playground.

For paddle enthusiasts Givhans Ferry State Park lies at the end of the Edisto River Canoe and Kayak Trail (ERCK) that begins at Colleton State Park on the Edisto River and ends at Givhans Ferry State Park. The Edisto River is the longest free flowing black water river in North America and travels from its headwaters near Saluda to the Atlantic Ocean. Tannic acid colors the Edisto River dark but, in reality, it is pure and clear. The entire ERCK Water Trail, sixty-two miles in length, begins at Green Pond Church Landing near Smoaks and ends at Lowndes Landing

just below Givhans Ferry park. All of the ERCK trail is popular with paddle enthusiasts, however, the trail section between Colleton State Park and Givhans Ferry State Park is easier to access and paddle and most widely utilized. There is a nice paved riverside put-in site for canoes, kayaks, and tubers beside the park's sandy swim beach.

Fishing is good on the river, too, and visitors can rent rods and reels at the park office or bring their own to fish off the banks. Fishing boats can access the river at a boat dock about three miles from the park and at several other nearby ramps. Anglers can catch bream, catfish, and redbreast sunfish. Messervy Landing is the closest boat dock but other docks like Mars Old Field are conveniently close to get to also.

Beyond the park office, playground, and beach on the river is a loop road leading back into the park's campground. There are 25 sites in the camp-

ground with water and electric, some for RVs, and tent camping sites. The campground has restrooms with hot showers, an outside shower for tubers, and a dump station. The road that loops through the campground and others around the park are also nice for walking and biking.

At the end of the road beyond the camping area is another large pavilion and beyond that the other end of the River Bluff Nature Trail. At the road's end is a second smaller pavilion, a picnic area and the gated entrance to the park's Primitive Campground. This is a big camping area where organized groups, like Scouts or church groups, with up to 100 people can camp. The camping area has nearby restroom facilities, central water, and a nice fire ring. The quiet roadway leading back to the campground also makes a nice short trail walk.

Back near the entrance of the park continue past the Welcome Station to follow the road around to the park's cabins. There are four nice cabins, built by the CCC, that sit on a quiet deadend road on a bluff overlooking the river. All have two bedrooms and are completely furnished with pretty screened in porches looking out through the trees and down to the Edisto River below. A trail leads from the cabins down the hillside on wooden steps and along the river to the swim beach—a pretty short trail in the park to explore, even if you're not staying in the cabins.

Givhans Ferry is a great park to visit or stay at for a vacation. For a day trip not far from the park, north on Hwy 61, kids will love visiting the Bee City Interactive Petting Zoo and Honey Farm.

The state park is also close to restaurants and shopping in nearby Summerville, near Cypress Garden at Moncks Corner, Charles Towne Landing State Park, and not far from many major tourist attractions around the Charleston area.

Colleton State Park

Lowcountry - Colleton County
Park Address: 147 Wayside Lane, Walterboro, SC 29488
Park Size: 35 acres   Month Visited: August
Directions: From I-95 south, take Exit 68 to Hwy 61 East. Follow
61/Augusta Hwy to crossing of Hwy 15. Turn left on Hwy 15 and
travel 0.3 miles to park entrance on left..

Park Description:

Colleton State Park is the smallest park in the state park system. It opened in 1944, and despite its small size is very popular with visitors, locals, and with paddlers and anglers, since it sits on the Edisto River. The park is only fifteen minutes from Walterboro's shops, stores, and restaurants and less than ten minutes from Interstate 95.

After entering the park, drive to the visitor center and office on the left, with its bright red rocking chairs on the side porch. When open, the office has nice restrooms and a small gift shop and you can talk to the ranger about things to do and see in the park and around the area. Across from the park is a spacious, well-equipped playground area for children with swings, slides, picnic tables, and a small pavilion.

Directly behind the office is the Cypress Swamp Nature Trail. This short, 0.3-miles trail leads through the woods on an easy pathway for all ages and across a boardwalk through a cypress swamp area to the Edisto River. You'll

see cypress stumps and tapered, pointed cypress knees sticking out of the brackish waters, amid wetlands grasses, tall bald cypress trees, and other vegetation. A brochure available at the park office corresponds to the eighteen numbered signs along the trail, identifying trees, ferns, and plants. At an intersection in the trail before arriving at the boardwalk, a second trail swings right to travel along the

river for about a mile to a canoe dock at the back end of the park.

After walking down the trail, drive to the end of the park's main road to the campground. Twenty-five campsites are scattered around a loop road with restrooms and hot showers, grills, picnic tables, and a dump station. The campsites are for RVs or tent camping and all have water and electric. Some can accommodate RVS up to 20 or 40 feet. Not far down the road is a primitive campground area for small groups. Trails from both campgrounds lead down to the river and to the put-in dock for canoes and kayaks. Swimming is allowed on the river as is fishing. Campers and visitors can get loaner rods and reels at the park office if they did not bring their own. Anglers catch bream, catfish, and redbreast sunfish on the river, and for more serious fishing by boat, there is a good public boat landing just across the river from the park.

There is also a rustic brown recreation building or rental cabin at the back of the campground. This cabin has two sets of bunks for

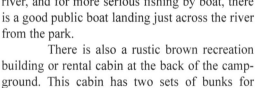

sleeping, but no indoor running water, bathroom, or kitchen, and if rented, all cooking must be done outside. Kayak and canoe enthusiasts often like this cabin for a simple stop over spot while padding the river. Colleton State Park is the unofficial headquarters for the Edisto River Canoe and Kayak (ERCK) trail. The popular 23-mile ERCK water trail to Givhans Ferry State Park begins here and kayakers and canoeists love paddling this section of the river. For those who don't bring their own boats, two nearby private outfitters offer rentals.

Fort Moultrie National Historic Park

Lowcountry - Charleston County
Park Address: 1214 Middle Street, Sullivan's Island, SC 29842
Park Size: 5.3 acres   Month Visited: August
Directions: Following I-26 into downtown Charleston, turn onto
Hwy 17 and cross the Cooper River on the Arthur Ravenel Jr.
Bridge. Swing right after crossing onto Coleman Avenue, staying
right into Hwy 702. Follow Hwy 702 and turn right on Middle
Street. Drive down Middle Street to the Fort and park signs.

Park Description:

Fort Moultrie, a well-preserved historic military site, was originally
built in 1776 to protect Charleston from the British during the Revolutionary
War (1775-1783). The Royal Navy attacked the fort on June 28, 1776, but after
a nine-hour battle against William Moultrie and his men, the British ships were
forced to retire. The British intent was to take Charleston, and stamp out the
new war for independence started by the American colonies, but under Moultrie's command, his regiment fought courageously, saving the fort and protecting
Charleston.

Over the years following the Revolutionary War, the fort fell into disre-
pair and was then wiped out by a hurricane in 1804. A second fort was constructed in 1808 but then heavily damaged by Union forces in the Civil War. Eventu-

ally after the war in the 1870s, a third strong brick and mortar fort was built. This fort, modernized several times since, served as a defensive point in World War II and remained in the U.S. coastal defense system until finally deactivated. Now listed on the National Register of Historic Places the fort is preserved and maintained by the National Park system for all to visit and enjoy.

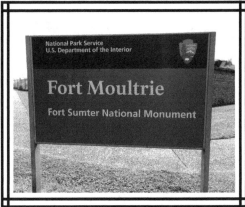

When you arrive at the Fort, first turn into the large free parking lot behind the visitor center. Inside the center is a park office, gift shop and bookstore, as well as a museum with artifacts and informative displays telling about Fort Moultrie's history. The visitor center also offers a free 20-minute orientation film depicting the fort's history. Guided tours of the fort are available at set hours for a fee or visitors can do self-guided tours using the park's brochure. We took the self-guided tour, with the fort's interior closed at our visit, and we enjoyed discovering the park at our leisure.

Begin exploring Fort Moultrie's grounds by walking down the sidewalk path behind the visitor center. The walkway leads by several informative signs, including one about Major General Moultrie, and then on to a fenced marker at his gravesite. Beyond that point is a shady picnic area on the Charleston Harbor and a long pier reaching out into the water. You can sit on the benches on the pier to look out across the lovely harbor views and watch the boats passing by. After looping back on this walkway, we headed across the road to the fort. On tours of the fort, given by park rangers, you will learn more history of the fort and see cannons, guns, batteries, bunkers, and a restored underground command center. You can also walk up to the control post tower, worth the stairs, for great views across the harbor to Fort Sumter.

Outside the fort, a wonderful walking trail leads in a long loop around the back of the fort to many interesting points, with kiosks and

signs providing information about the sites along the way. Starting on the left of the fort, we passed the control post tower and then stopped at a long row of big cannons, a treat to see up close. Nearby a side pathway led to displays telling about the H.L. Hunley, a Confederate submarine that set out to attack a Union warship in 1865 during the Civil War. After ramming a torpedo into the ship, the Hunley disappeared and was never found, leaving behind a mystery still unsolved. More signs nearby tell about the Endicott defense system, powerhouse, gun battery, and water supply area for the soldiers. The concrete gun battery, called the Jasper Battery, is named for Sergeant William Jasper, an artilleryman in the Revolutionary War battle at the fort. Jasper distinguished himself by picking up the American flag, after the flagpole was shot down, and taking it to the top of the fort to bravely hold it there until a new flagpole could be erected.

We loved all the stories like these we discovered about South Carolina and U.S. history while wandering in the buildings and grounds at Fort Moultrie. Another fun discovery was learning that the famous writer and poet Edgar Allen Poe was stationed at Fort Moultrie as a young soldier in the 1800s. He served in the Army under the assumed name Edgar A. Perry for five years. As a clerk, Poe was probably one of the few enlisted men of his time who could read and write, and he eventually rose from the rank of Private to Sgt. Major. Poe's memories of the Carolina coast later played a part in some of his books, and today a street and several sites are named in Poe's memory on Sullivan's Island.

As we continued the last part of our park walk, the trail wound around to more cannons and informative signs and to a grassy trail leading down to the beach. The beach is quiet here and a nice place for a stroll. We watched ships

164

on the harbor and looked across to Fort Sumter before winding around the south side of the fort to finish our walking tour. Fort Moultrie, a great park to visit, is rich with history and is the only area in the National Park System where the entire 171-year history of U.S. coastal defense can be traced.

History Note:

Major General William Moultrie (1730-1805), a famous Revolutionary War hero and Continental officer, was born and educated in Charleston. In 1749 after marrying Demaris Elizabeth de St. Julien, a wealthy woman whose family owned a large plantation, Moultrie became a planter, soon adding a second plantation. Also active in the government of South Carolina, Moultrie was elected to the Carolina Commons House of Assembly

in 1752 and appointed a captain of a South Carolina militia in 1760. A staunch supporter of the revolutionary cause, Moultrie and 435 men, in 1776 at the beginning of the war, valiantly defended the small fort he had built on Sullivan's Island against 2200 British troops and nine British warships. Against what most considered impossible odds, Moultrie and his men prevailed and prevented the

British Navy from invading Charleston. A hero of South Carolina, Moultrie was later made a Brigadier General, the last man to receive that rank during the Revolutionary War, and he also became a SC governor and state senator. Fort Moultrie was named in his honor and the South Carolina flag today is based on the flag Moultrie designed and flew at the Battle of Sullivan's Island.

Charles Pinckney National Historic Site

Lowcountry - Charleston County
Park Address: 1254 Long Point Rd, Mt. Pleasant, SC 29464
Park Size: 28 acres   Month Visited: August
Directions: From I-26 south, in Charleston take Arthur J. Ravenel
Bridge over the Cooper River on Hwy 17. Follow Hwy 17 north.
Follow to Long Point Road on left. Continue a half-mile to park
sign and entrance on left.

Park Description:

The Charles Pinckney National Historic Site, on the National Register of Historic Places, offers an opportunity to learn about the life of one of South Carolina's well-known public figures. The park lies six miles north of Charleston in Mt. Pleasant and the small acreage is a remnant of the original 715-acre Pinckney rice and indigo plantation. On the grounds are a historic home, a small shed, placards and markers to tell about different historic sites, a nice picnic area under the trees, a pretty covered pavilion with restrooms, and a walking trail.

The centerpiece of the park is the Snee Farmhouse, a large cape-cod style house built in the 1820s and now the lone structure of any size remaining on the property. The Snee Farmhouse was not actually built by the Pinckneys, as the family sold their entire plantation property in 1817. Inside the farmhouse, built by the second owners of the plantation, are a museum, small souvenir store, and a visitor center, where you can pick up a park brochure and a trail map and learn about the park's history. In a side room you can watch the 17-minute film about Pinckney's life called *Forgotten Founder*. The park also has two other films available if you have time to view them: a 24-minute film called *Birth of the Constitution* and an 11-minute film titled *Founding Brothers: Sides of Slavery*. Museum exhibits are available to tour in three additional rooms of the house. The museum rooms contain artifacts, paintings, maps, documents, and information panels about South Carolina history and the

Pinckney family. You will also learn here about archeological digs done on the property and how these have helped archeologists and historians learn more about other buildings that used to be a part of the Pinckney plantation. Digs have located the sites of former kitchen and slave buildings and found old items, dishes, and tools.

While visiting the park, take time to walk the half-mile Nature Trail that starts at the visitor center. It follows a grassy path through a field area where slave quarters used to be and then winds through a tidal wetland under moss-draped oaks and over a boardwalk to an overlook of the Wampacheone Creek. As the trail loops back to the farmhouse you'll see a model of a rice trunk used to control the flow of water between rice paddies.

History Note:

Charles Pinckney (1757-1824) born to a wealthy family in Charleston before the Revolutionary War, was well educated, became a lawyer at twenty-one and soon moved into political service. Even before his marriage to Mary Eleanor Laurens in 1794 he was a delegate to the Federal Constitutional Congress, helped, in part, to draft the U.S. Constitution, and was a signer of the ratified Constitution. Pinckney served as an ambassador to Spain, was a four time Governor of South Carolina, a U.S. Senator, and a member of the U.S. House of Representatives. Since the Pinckney family owned several plantations as

well as a home in downtown Charleston, Charles and his wife and children used the Snee Farm plantation mostly as a summer home.

Santee State Park

Lowcountry - Orangeburg County
Park Address: 251 State Park Road, Santee, SC 29412
Park Size: 2500 acres   Month Visited: October
Directions: From I-95, take Santee Exit heading north on Hwy 6.
Just past Santee Golf Course turn right onto State Park Road at
park sign. Follow to lake and visitor center.

Park Description:

This a beautiful state park on the shore of Lake Marion. The park has two campgrounds, rental cabins, two boat docks, a fishing pier, hiking and biking trails on a scenic property. After entering the park, stay on the west park road and follow it to the Park Office and Visitor Center. This is a large facility with park brochures, maps, a gift shop, and an Interpretive Center with wildlife exhibits and educational information. Picnic areas, a children's playground, and several pavilions lie across the street, and behind the center are glorious views of Lake Marion.

Lake Marion is the largest lake in South Carolina, covering 110,000 acres and touching into five counties, with 315 miles of shoreline. The lake was created in 1941 by the construction of the eight mile long Santee Dam and named for Revolutionary War hero

Frances Marion. The lake—and park—are a water-lovers paradise and the park is popular with boaters and anglers year round. Bass, crappie, and other tournaments are held at Santee at different times of the year. Among the fish caught on Lake Marion are catfish, bass, crappie, bluegill, bream, trout, and stripers. Around the park area wildlife abounds, too, with turtles, deer, and a wide variety of birds like

snowy egrets, owls, and hawks. Alligators are often seen in the lake, as well, some up to ten to twelve feet long. To spot even more wildlife the Santee National Wildlife Refuge, operated by the U.S. Fish and Wildlife Service, is located on the north shore across from the park and has its own visitor center, educational exhibits, walking trails, and observation areas.

The road beyond the visitor center leads to the park's thirty rental cabins, all rondette cabins, and The Village Round Community Center building. Ten of the park's cabins, the Pier Cabins, sit on two piers overlooking the lake—providing a unique lodging experience. The other twenty, the Shoreline Cabins are along

a quiet winding road looking out over Lake Marion. All have views of the lake with trails down to the water for launching canoes and kayaks or for fishing. All cabins are completely furnished with two bedrooms and picnic tables, and the Shoreline Cabins with porches, grills, and patio areas.

Across from the cabins one of the park's hiking trails wanders for almost a mile through the woods, the Oak Pinolly Trail. The park has ten miles of hiking and biking trails. A long 7.5-miles biking trail winds in a loop between the east and west sides of the park, along the lakeside and through the woods with cut-over trails, called the White Trail and the Red Trail, along the way. At the park's east end is the interesting Sinkhole Pond Trail. This 0.75-miles trail is especially scenic. It wanders through the woods and over bridges across a pond or inlet of the lake. Along the way is one of the limestone sinkhole areas often formed in this area when the ground drops in or sinks toward underground caverns. An informative kiosk along the trail explains how sinkholes are formed.

Not far from the Visitor Center is the Cypress Landing park store with a long fishing pier reaching out behind it. The park store has bait, tackle, snacks, ice cream, gifts, souvenir items, firewood, and a Wifi lounge. Beside it is one of the park's boat ramps and there are picnic tables scattered along the banks looking out over the lake. Books and games can be checked out at the store, fishing licenses bought, and a large-screen television enjoyed. In addition, two-hour narrated tours of the lake area can be taken with the Fisheagle Adventures Boat Tour company located beside the park store. The tour takes visitors out in a pontoon

tour boat to see at closer range the cypress trees still growing in the lake, water tupelo, wetland wading birds, osprey nests, and other wildlife.

Not far from the store, one of the park's two campgrounds winds along a figure-eight loop by the lake. The Cypress View Campground has about fifty sites with electric and water, but no sewer, two restrooms with showers, and a dump station. All are close to the lake for walks along the shore or fishing. Heading back toward the park entrance area and driving to the East Side of the park leads to the park's other campground, the Lakeshore Campground. This second campground, also on the lake, has over one-hundred sites on several interlinking roads, a recreation building, several restrooms with showers, and a dump station. The larger of the two campgrounds, Lakeshore's sites also have electric and water but no sewer. Also within the campground are designated tent sites and on a side road before the campground entrance is a primitive camping area for organized groups. The camp area, large enough for groups up to one hundred, has its own restroom facilities.

A left side road before the campground road leads out to a peninsula with several pavilions, a picnic area and second playground, and access to the Sinkhole Trail and the Mountain Bike Trail, which can be enjoyed by hikers, also. Near Santee State Park are several fine golf courses and in the town of Santee are a variety of restaurants, shops, and grocery stores. We really enjoyed this park and its proximity to the town of Santee as well, where we stayed while exploring the Midlands area.

Myrtle Beach

PEE DEE SOUTH CAROLINA STATE PARK
INDEX

PEE DEE

South Carolina
PARKS

Cheraw

Hampton Plantation

Lee

Little Pee Dee

Myrtle Beach State Park

Pee Dee - Horry County
Park Address: 4401 Kings Highway, Myrtle Beach, SC 29575
Park Size: 312 acres   Month Visited: October
Directions: From I-95 south, travel from Florence via Hwy 76 thru
Marion and southeast on Hwy 501 to S. Kings Hwy/Business 17.
Follow south to entrance to Myrtle Beach State Park on left.

Park Description:

       Since we hadn't visited the Myrtle Beach area in many years, we en-
joyed traveling a highway section down the Grand Strand, a 60 mile-long beach
area extending from North Myrtle Beach at the NC border to Winyah Bay near
Georgetown. It's hard to believe as you drive down this route, with high-rise ho-
tels stretching in every direction, that before 1901 this area was essentially undeveloped wilderness. Early beach front lots sold then for only $25 each while
today Myrtle Beach is the leading tourist destination in South Carolina, attracting
over 14 million visitors a year. It is a busy, packed metropolitan area with over
10,000 hotel rooms and more than one hundred golf courses. Within this hectic,
highly populated tourist area sits Myrtle Beach State Park, a quiet, green, non-
commercial, peaceful oasis. The park has beautiful natural scenery, old growth
forest, woodlands, sandy trails, and a one-mile undeveloped stretch of beach on
the Atlantic coastline.

Myrtle Beach was the first state park to open in South Carolina in 1936 and was built, as were many of the state's parks, by the Civilian Conservation Corps (CCC). A long drive winds from the park entrance through woodlands to the fee station and then on to the park office, a nice spot to stop for information and a park map. Just beyond the park office on the left is a parking lot, picnic area and

pavilion. A side trails leads to the park's Activity and Nature Center. The center offers science programs and events for visitors and inside the center you'll find interactive displays, an aquarium and live reptiles. On the center grounds are educational signs, a butterfly garden with flowers, birdhouses, and natural sculptures. A recreational area nearby offers bocce ball, horseshoes and other activities with equipment available at the ranger station.

Across the street from this area is the beginning of one of the park's trails, the half mile Sculptured Oak Nature Trail. The easy sandy trail follows to a pond or down to the beach. It connects, also, to the Yaupon Nature Trail, a 0.4-miles trail that starts at the south end of the beach. You can combine the Sculptured Oak, Yaupon, and Pond

Trail for a longer 2.5-miles hike and enjoy informative signs and rest benches along the way. The park's other trail is a Boardwalk Trail near the ocean and beach pavilions. All trails are flat and easy to walk and pass by many wax myrtle trees that the park and town are named for.

Continuing on the main road leads directly to the Atlantic Ocean and the beach. There are several parking lots here with access to the beach, picnic tables and pavilions, the Pier Store, and the park's long fishing pier reaching out into the ocean. The park has seven pavilions, which can be reserved and rented by the day for groups. Inside the Pier Store you can get snacks, fishing supplies, bait and tackle, souvenirs, and buy a fishing pass to fish off the long 650-foot pier that juts far out into the Atlantic Ocean. Some of the most common fish caught are whiting, drum, spot, sea trout, and mackerel. Surf fishing is also allowed from the beach but only in the seasons when no lifeguards and crowds are present. Even if you don't fish just walking out on this tall, wooden pier to enjoy the views of the ocean and beach is fun.

Where the main road ends near the Pier Store, the road splits, to run south along the beach in one direction and north along the beach in the other. For access to the beach and the ocean, the Myrtle Beach State Park has built lovely boardwalks over the dunes and leading down to the beach at ten points along the park's one-mile stretch of beachfront. There are also nice restrooms, pavilions, picnic tables, and several playgrounds for children scattered along the beach area. Even at our visit in October many people were enjoying sitting under their umbrellas, walking along the beach, visiting in groups, or fishing.

After exploring the South park area, the beach and the trails, we headed north to check out the campground and cabin areas. A picturesque winding road leads back to the park's six cabins, all in a quiet section of the park on a deadend street. The cabins are all large with two, three, or four bedrooms and each has a full kitchen and a pretty screened porch.

The nearby campground is a large one and was nearly full of campers the day we visited. There are 140 sites with electric and water, 138 more full sites with sewer and 30 tent sites. There is a registration center, ranger station, and store just inside the campground entrance that offers camping supplies, drinks, snacks, firewood, and some grocery items. The campground is laid out in circular streets with multiple restroom areas with hot showers, a laundry, playground, recycling bins, dumpster, and dump station.

With the Myrtle Beach State Park in such a large metropolitan area there are a wealth of amusements nearby to enjoy, many restaurants to try, tourist attractions to visit, golf courses, gardens, historic homes, shops and shopping centers. The nearby area has several museums, theatres with live shows, a wildlife preserve with safari tours, a winery, and a multitude of annual events that draw big crowds like the fall Shag Dancing Festival. If you enjoy a park in a busy area with lots to see and do, this is it!

Huntington Beach State Park

Pee Dee - Georgetown County
Park Address: 16148 Ocean Highway, Murrells Inlet, SC 29576
Park Size: 2500 acres   Month Visited: October
Directions: From I-95 south, travel from Florence on Hwy 76 thru
Marion and southeast on Hwy 501 to S. Kings Hwy/Bus 17 into
Ocean Hwy. Follow south to park entrance on left.

Park Description:

      This stunning park stands out in memory as one of our favorite coastal parks. The entrance road winds through the woods and then across a long causeway between a fresh water lagoon and a saltwater marsh. On the causeway are two observation decks, which can be reached by a walkway from the parking area at the causeway's end. The short walk to the observation points offers lovely views of the marsh and the lagoon called Mullet Pond. A second path from the parking lot leads out onto the pond on a long boardwalk, for more pretty views. Both walks hint right away at the unique beauty of this park.

      The road to the right beyond the causeway leads to the ranger station, a gift shop, picnic area, beach access path, campgrounds, and the Antalaya estate the park is known for. At the big park office, store and gift shop, visitors can pick up maps and information, souvenirs, snacks, groceries, firewood and walk up a series of steps to an observation deck. Behind the office, the one-fourth mile Kerrigan Nature Trail leads on a forested trail to a second boardwalk extending into

the lagoon. Across the street from the office, a broad, paved walkway leads through a shady, scenic park with picnic tables, pavilions, restrooms, and out to the beach and the Atlantic Ocean. The park includes three miles of beautiful beach area, the northern end more remote and also a bird sanctuary.

Huntington has two campgrounds, the larger North Campground and a new smaller campground south of the office. The South Campground offers a short concrete road with sites for large RVs, and has a comfort station, laundry, and beach access. The North Campground has a diversity of sites for both RVs and tents, and a recreation building, all tucked under shady trees on two scenic loop roads. There are a total of 173 sites with water & electric, 66 with full sewer hookup, and both have access to restrooms with hot showers, a dump station, play areas, and nice beach access paths. There are also six rustic tent sites and a primitive group camping area,

Near the park office and campgrounds is the home of Archer and Anna Huntington, the home leased along with 2500 acres to South Carolina in 1960 for use as a state park. The Huntingtons' distinctive house, built in a Moorish design, was named Antalaya (Ah-ta-LIE-yah). More like a castle in appearance, the home has thirty rooms laid out around a central courtyard, with work studios, a kennel, animal enclosures, and a small museum. The name Antalaya means "watch tower" in Spanish, the name coined from the 40-foot water tower, rising high to look out over land and sea in the middle of the home's courtyard. There are informative plaques throughout Antalaya and visitors can take a tour of the castle's interior for a small fee or wander the walkways and grounds for free.

Driving into the north section of the park on Jetty Road leads to the Nature Center.

Inside are interactive exhibits and displays about the area's coastal environment. The center offers weekly programs and activities, and beside the Nature Center is another of the park's trails, a short boardwalk trail leading into the saltwater marsh. The park, also a wildlife refuge and bird sanctuary, is home to hundreds of species of marsh and sea birds and many can be spotted here off the boardwalk.

Beyond the Nature Center at the end of the road is another picnic and pavilion area and the beginning of the one mile Sandpiper Pond Nature Trail, an in-and-out trail (2 miles RT). Walking a short distance down the trail leads to a large observation deck looking across picturesque Sandpiper Pond. From the parking lot, a pathway follows out to the beach. A walk north down the beach for a little over a mile, leads to a jetty extending into the ocean. The jetty, a manmade rocky structure, built to protect the beach at the park's end, reaches for one-fourth mile out into the sea and has a wide paved walkway across the top. Anglers love to come here to surf fish off the rocks or walkway and visitors enjoy walking far out to the jetty's end. The views are glorious from the jetty and it's fun to watch all the boats zipping in and out of Murrell's Inlet. Kayak and canoe enthusiasts like launching their boats at nearby Oyster Landing in the park to paddle down Oaks Creek to the jetty and the ocean.

Huntington Beach State Park is a delight for bikers, too. Cyclists love riding the quiet roadways in this park and biking the long paved section of the Waccamaw Neck Bikeway that passes directly through the park. The entire length of the bikeway runs for 18.6 miles from Garden City through Murrells Inlet and the park to Pawleys Island. For all who enjoy biking, camping, hiking, picnicking, surf fishing or just lazing at the beach, this park is a gem you won't want to miss.

History Note:

The Huntington Beach State Park and the Brookgreen Gardens across the street from it are the legacy of Archer Huntington (1870-1955) and his wife Anna Hyatt Huntington (1876-1973). The couple met and married in midlife, Anna already a well-known, successful sculptor and Archer a wealthy industrialist and philanthropist. When Anna contracted tuberculosis, the New York couple searched for land in the South where they could build a winter home in a milder climate to aid Anna's recovery. In the midst of the Great Depression (1929-1933), they purchased a vast tract of 6,600 acres of mostly undeveloped wilderness near Murrells Inlet, SC. Hiring mostly local labor, they built Antalaya, developed nature preserves,

and created Brookgreen Gardens, which displays fine sculpture in a garden setting, including many of Anna's pieces. The state park, lands and garden, are now National Historic Landmarks and on the National Register of Historic Places.

Hampton Plantation State Historic Site

Pee Dee - Georgetown County
Park Address: 1950 Rutledge Road, McClellanville. SC 29458
Park Size: 274 acres   Month Visited: October
Directions: From coastal Highway 17 south of McClellanville, SC, cross the South Santee River bridge, and watch for Rutledge Road/State Hwy 10. Turn right and follow to state park sign and entrance on right.

Park Description:

 Hampton Plantation, built in the 1700s, was a prosperous rice plantation before the Civil War. The site once covered 2000 acres of land along the Santee River and the home and grounds still serve as an interpretive example of the rice cultivation era. The beautiful two and a half storied white Georgian plantation home has twelve rooms, over 10,000 square feet, porches front and back, a kitchen house behind the main house, and is now on the list of National Historic Landmarks and the National Register of Historic Places. A long ballroom is the largest room inside the house where the family hosted banquets, balls, and social gatherings. Long avenues lead to the home from the front and side and many trails wind through the plantation site, down to the Santee River, and to the family cemetery. Notables such as Francis Marion and George Washington visited the plantation and a large oak tree in front of the home is called the George Washington Oak because Washington suggested the tree should not be cut down. If you look carefully you can still see the family dinner bell between two high branches of the tree.

Begin your exploration of the plantation site at the visitor center, which includes the park office and a gift shop. Pick up brochures and an informative map here so you can find your way to the interesting spots around the Hampton Plantation grounds. To the left of the visitor center next to the park restrooms stands the old Alston house chimney. Owned by descendants of Prince and

Sue Altson, the chimney is the only remaining part of one of the slave homes on the property.

Slaves maintained the plantation's work before the Civil War and between 1770 and 1820 Hampton had about a hundred slaves. They were responsible for building the family and slave homes, buildings, roads, and the intricate systems of dams, drains, and ditches needed to irrigate the rice fields. The plantation at its height produced 3000 pounds of rice a year. On the two-mile Hampton Plantation Nature Trail are remnants of the rice planting operation, a rice dyke, rice trunk, and informational plaques. Visitors can also see the foundations of early slave dwellings on the property and a slave cemetery, called the Sam Hill cemetery. Some families like the Boykins and Alstons stayed on as tenant farmers after the Civil War and worked and lived at Hampton until its sale to the state.

Although the interior of the plantation home is not furnished, tours can be taken of the home at scheduled times. Touring the interior of the house allows visitors to see the fine architecture and old grandeur still evident throughout, high ceilings, beautiful hardwood floors, lavish stairwells, old fireplaces,

and decorative cornices. Behind the main house is the separate kitchen house where meals were prepared and brought to the main house, remnants of the family garden, pathways down to the river, and plaques telling about the family and the nearby family burial grounds. The stories about the home and the families who lived here are rich ones, and learning about the different families who made their lives at the plantation, like the Horrys, Pinckneys, and the Rutledges, link into the history of the area and how plantations that produced rice, cotton, and indigo grew and thrived in that time. Nearby Georgetown, about sixteen miles away, was the center of rice production in the Carolina country. Many historic buildings still remain in what is termed the Rice Museum complex around Front Street, including the Rice Museum, an Old Market Building, Town Clock, Hardware Building, Maritime Museum Gallery and more – a nice side trip where you can learn more about these early times in the Carolinas.

After the Civil War, the Hampton Plantation was used mostly for farming and as a hunting retreat and family homesite. The Rutledge family sold Hampton Plantation and its remaining property to the state of South Carolina in 1971 and in 1982 it was opened to the public as a state park.

History Note:

Archibald Hamilton Rutledge (1883-1973), an American poet and educator, was the last of the Rutledge family to live at Hampton Plantation. Times were

hard in the South after the Civil War, but Rutledge attained scholarships to attend college. After earning bachelors (1904) and masters (1907) degrees, he went to work in the English Department of Mercersburg Academy in Pennsylvania where he met and married Florence Hart and stayed on to teach for thirty-two years. A brilliant and multi-faceted man, Rutledge was a prolific writer, authored over fifty books and had many stories, poems, and articles published in national magazines, most memorializing his South Carolina home and memories.

In 1934 Rutledge was named the state's first Poet Laureate, was nominated for a Pulitzer Prize in 1960, and received seventeen honorary degrees and thirty medals for his work. Throughout his academic years he, Florence, and their three sons returned to spend every summer at Hampton. After his wife's death, Rutledge retired in 1937, returned to the plantation he'd inherited from his father, and married Alice Lucas, his old high school sweetheart. Finding the plantation in a poor state on his return, Rutledge worked hard for many years to restore the estate and his book *Home By the River* (1941) tells about the plantation he so loved.

185

Poinsett State Park

Pee Dee - Sumter County
Park Address: 6660 Poinsett Park Road, Wedgefield, SC 29168
Park Size: 2500 acres   Month Visited: October
Directions: From Interstate 95, take Exit 119 to Hwy 261 NW
through Paxville and Pineville, swinging north into the Manchester State Forest. Turn left on Hwy 63/Poinsett Park Road and follow into the park.

Park Description:

Tucked in the Manchester State Forest, Poinsett is a delightful park to visit. Although set in the Pee Dee area near the middle of the state, the park has a surprisingly mountainous terrain, and yet within it are also wetland areas with cypress trees and Spanish moss. Poinsett, which opened in 1936, was one of the early parks built by three Civilian Conservation Corps (CCC) camps, including a World War I group of veterans and an African-American company. You'll notice CCC handiwork at the entry of the park as you pass through two old rock walls and by one of the picturesque shelters built by the CCC using coquina, a local limestone rock composed partly of shells and fossil debris. Beyond the entrance the main road threads through woodlands and along Shanks Creek to end at a parking area. To the left you'll see the beautiful stone visitor center and gift shop, with its attached meeting room that features a large rustic fireplace and long windows

looking across the lake. The park office, nearby pavilions, cabins, recreation building, rock walls, bridges, and shelters, all built by the CCC, were listed on the National Register of Historic Places in 2016.

Beside the ten-acre lake, named Levi Mill Pond, is a sandy swim beach and a boathouse where canoes, paddleboats, kayaks, and jon boats can be rented. Also by the lake are picnic tables, pavilions and a nice children's playground. Near the park office, be sure to walk west of the office a short distance to the dam and spillway. At the dam, follow the gray rock stairs downhill to a wooden bridge crossing the waterfall spillway about midway. This is a lovely spot and nearby you can see the ruins of the old gristmill that an early settler named Levi built to impound water in the 1700s before the American Revolution. Levi Mill Pond is named for him and Poinsett Park is named to honor South Carolina native Joel Roberts Poinsett (1779-1851), a botanist, a member of the South Carolina legislature, and the first ambassador to Mexico.

From the spillway area, one of the most popular park trails begins by winding its way around the lake in a loop hike. The full Coquina Trail is about 1.5

miles in length but visitors often take other trails that connect into Coquina to extend their hike or to avoid the swamp area at the end of the lake. This wetlands trail section often floods, washing out the boardwalk bridges. For a shorter one-mile roundtrip walk, simply follow the Coquina Trail for a half-mile to the Coquina Shelter, a rustic CCC shelter tucked away in the woods, and then return on the same path.

Poinsett State Park has a network of 25.6-miles of hiking and biking trails winding out of different areas of the park and even linking in with the Palmetto Trail, the long foot and bike trail extending across South Carolina for over three hundred miles. A map of all the trails is available at the park office and online. Some of the trails are easy to access from the main areas of the park. Others are interior trails linking off other trails. Several of the more popular trails start near the parking area. Besides the Coquina Trail, we hiked a piece of the 3.9-miles Knot Trail behind the lake, the 1.0-mile Splice Trail that starts across from the park office, a section of the 1.8-miles Scout Trail starting at the Overlook Shelter parking area, and a portion of the Whippoorwill Trail that begins on the main road by Cabin Creek near the park cabins. Bikers love these trails and often drive from nearby Sumter or Columbia to ride. In caution, plan to bring bug spray to best enjoy all the trails.

A side road, not far from the park office, leads uphill to an overlook shelter, pavilion, and trail access points and then on to the park's campground area. The campground's shady loop road has 50 campsites in total, 24 standard sites with electric and 26 rustic tent sites. All have access to two bathhouse facilities, a nice recreation building, and a dump station. On a nearby side road is a group camping area as well, with central water and restrooms, ideal for organized groups up to 200 people.

Down the main road, closer to the park entrance, another scenic side road leads to the park's five historic cabins built 75 years ago by the CCC. All have one or two bedrooms, pretty screen porches, patios and picnic tables, and can sleep two to seven persons. The cabins sit on a quiet and shaded street, an ideal spot for a getaway into nature. Be sure to add this interesting park on your "to visit" list. It has over 337 species of flowering plants, 65 species of shrubs, many types of trees, a wide variety of birds and wildlife, a network of lovely trails, and scenic beauty you will love and long remember.

H Cooper Black State Park
Memorial Field Trial & Recreation Area

Pee Dee - Chesterfield County
Park Address: 279 Sporting Dog Trail, Cheraw, SC 29620
Park Size: 7000 acres   Month Visited: October
Directions: From Hwy 25 near Cheraw, take Hwy 1 south for appx 5.6 miles; turn left on Society Hill Rd. After 4.5 miles, turn right on Cooper Rd for 13 miles to Sporting Dog Trail Road and park.

Park Description:

H Cooper Black, added to the SC state park system in 1994, is one of the most unique parks in the state. The park, a peaceful, remote property with 7000 acres of fields and longleaf pine forest, was originally part of the Sand Hills State Forest. Named for Dr. Henry Cooper Black, Jr (1939-1993), a surgeon by vocation and an avid sport hunting and outdoor enthusiast by avocation, the park is the only state park available for field trials and retriever competitions at the state and national level. The park is also an equestrian event center with a show ring and barns and more than twenty miles of trails.

After entering the park, drive in to the park office, which can be found at one end of a 24-stall equestrian stable. Needed information about the park, brochures, maps, and gift items are available here. Near the office is a fenced children's playground, restrooms, picnic area, horse corrals and the equestrian show ring. Across from the show ring is the park's campground. A total of 27 campsites are available with water and electric, some with sewer, and suitable for RVs. The park also has other campsite areas for tent and additional event camping. The equestrian friendly campsite also has 16 x 16 panel corrals by the campsites for horses, as well as grills, fire pits, comfort stations with hot showers, and a dump station.

Not far from the office is the park's meeting hall for indoor events, a nice-sized building with restrooms and a covered entry. Following the road leading around behind the meeting hall leads to Goose Pond, one of several ponds on the park grounds. This and the other ponds in the park, Mallard Pond and Griggs Pond, are great places for fishing as is 42-acre Campbells Lake on the west end of the park. The ponds and lake, all tucked along side roads or riding trails, are scenic and popular for bank fishing, dog training, and retriever events, and at Wood

Duck Pond is a covered picnic pavilion.

To the delight of equestrians, quiet sandy riding trails lattice throughout the park, providing a good place to ride in all seasons. All the trails are easy and flat, winding through the pine forest, open field areas, and alongside the ponds. Review sites name H Cooper Black as one of the most equestrian friendly parks in South Carolina and it is easy to see why they love this beautifully kept parkland. There is no better place, either, to catch a glimpse of some of the nation's finest horses and dogs at the park's competition events.

Competitions take precedence at H Cooper Black, and because of that it is important to check with the park about scheduled events prior to visiting as sometimes access to the park is limited or closed due to ongoing competitions, shows, or events. Additionally, H Cooper Black allows hunting during season for deer, turkey and other small game, and extra care should be taken during open seasons to wear appropriate orange blaze clothing for safety, and to comply with park regulations.

Cheraw State Park

Pee Dee - Chesterfield County
Park Address: 100 State Park Road, Cheraw, SC 29520
Park Size: 2361 acres   Month Visited: October
Directions: From Interstate 95 North, take Florence Exit 164 to
Hwy 52 North. Follow through Darlington and Society Hill, and
turn left at second park entrance sign on Cheraw State Park Road
after crossing Jasper Creek.

Park Description:

This beautiful park proved to be a favorite of ours. Cheraw State Park, built in the 1930s by the Civilian Conservation Corps, sprawls along two sides of 360-acre Lake Juniper and offers a broad array of amenities, camping, fishing, boating, hiking, horseback and biking trails, and an 18-hole golf course. The nearby town of Cheraw, only four to five miles away, provides additional places to visit while staying in or near the park. Cheraw, nicknamed "The Prettiest Town in Dixie," has historic sites, a museum, parks, and a Splash Island for kids. In addition the Carolina Sandhills National Wildlife Refuge is nearby with more hiking, biking, and fishing opportunities.

After entering the park follow the signage to the park office and visitor center, a long rustic building looking out across the lake with a lovely rock patio behind it. To either side of the office are restrooms and a bathhouse. A pathway from the park office leads directly down to a big sand beach on the lake, with recreation play areas, a playground, and picnic tables nearby. This is a gorgeous spot for a day on the lake and a local woman we visited with, while eating our picnic lunch, told us stories of her years coming to this park with her friends to swim and boat. A girlhood challenge was to swim the lake, which she remembered doing once she was older.

Along the lake are the park's two picnic shelters, both with beautiful views. In front of the larger pavilion the Boardwalk Trail begins, leading for a half mile around the side of Lake Juniper. The lake is a perfect spot for an afternoon of boating or fishing. A boat ramp can be found on the other side of the lake and at the park office peddle boats, canoes, kayaks, and small jon boats can be rented. A popular monthly activity, offered from March to October, is the Moonlight Canoe Event, where boaters travel the two and a half mile length of the lake.

Not far from the Cheraw office, a quiet loop road leads to the park's nine cabins, built by the CCC. All the fully-equipped cabins offer pretty screened porches, one to four bedrooms, kitchen and living areas, grills, picnic tables, and

are within walking distance of the lake. Near the cabin road is the park's large community building called the House on the Hill. With a large meeting room and kitchen, the rustic building can accommodate up to 60 people. The building, with a rich history, is a popular spot for meetings, weddings, and reunions.

Continuing west deeper into the park leads to Cheraw's 18-hole golf course. Golfers start their play at the big full-service pro shop, with a gift shop, snack grill, and scenic covered porches all around. The course, with a practice green and driving range, offers a championship layout and gently sloping greens in a park like setting. The course, a Certified Audubon International Wildlife Sanctuary, has been called "the best kept secret in South Carolina."

Beyond the golf course is the start of the Turkey Oak Trail. Hikers can enjoy walking the inner 2.0-mile nature loop or link to a second loop to hike the full 4.5-miles length of the trail. Turkey Oak is a mostly flat pathway through a quiet, peaceful pine woods, with crossings over seeps on wooden walkways. At the 2.0-mile point, the trail comes to a nice stream and a lookout across Lake Juniper. Hikers may spot turkeys, deer, hawks, and other wildlife and wildflowers in the spring. Cheraw also has a nine-mile mountain bike trail of rolling, sandy terrain through a longleaf pine forest. The bike trail starts off Highway 1 and winds through a remote section of the park. The trail is mostly flat but has some ups and downs to add biking challenge.

A second park road off Hwy 52 on the other side of Lake Juniper leads to the park's boat ramp and campground. The small but scenic campground has 17 campsites. Each site is packed gravel and has electric and water, a picnic table, fire ring, and grill. Trails wander down to the lakeside where campers can fish or

put their kayaks or canoes into the water. The campground can accommodate tents, trailers, and RVs up to 40 feet and has a comfort station, dump station, and a camp store. Although small, we loved this little campground and enjoyed visiting with campers there. A short walk leads to the south end of the Boardwalk Trail, which winds for a half mile along the lake, across a pretty bridge, dam and spillway—just a beautiful walk. The

road continuing beyond the campground winds back to the park's two large group camps, Camp Juniper and Camp Forest, which both used to be youth camps. There is also an equestrian camp area and a 6-mile horse trail called the John Finckley Memorial Horse Trail, that travels through a pine forest. There is really something for everyone at Cheraw and it is a scenic, diverse, and memorable park to visit.

Little Pee Dee State Park

Pee Dee - Dillon County
Park Address: 2400 Park Access Road, Dillon, SC, 29538
Park Size: 835 acres   Month Visited: October
Directions: From Interstate 95 North, take Dillon Exit 190. Follow Hwy 34 into and through Dillon to Hwy 9 southeast. Travel appx ten miles on Hwy 9 from Dillon to right on State Park Road and follow to park sign and entrance.

Park Description:

Little Pee Dee State Park is in a nice location, not far from Florence, South Carolina, and only a little over an hour from North Myrtle Beach and the coast. The route into the park from the interstate travels directly through the small historic town of Dillon. Established in 1888, Dillon offers local landmarks like the courthouse on Main, old train depot, original Dillon Theater, several historic churches, an Antebellum bed and breakfast built in 1903, and picturesque homes. The Little Pee Dee park is not far from the town or from its restaurants, stores, and shops, convenient for campers. In addition, about five miles north of Dillon in Hamer is Pedroland Park, an amusement park with a carousel, ferris wheel and other rides, two miniature golf courses, and a huge playground and picnic area.

An interesting fact about Little Pee Dee State Park is that one of the rare Carolina Bays lies within the park and the Heritage Preserve next to it. Carolina bays are mysterious geological depressions unique to the Atlantic coastal plain. They are surprising sights to see inland with their sweeps of white sands with low growing shrubs and trees like you'd expect at the coast. The bays usually cover a few acres, although some are larger, and have an oval or elliptical freshwater depression within them that fills up with water during rains. The bays, home to frogs, salamanders, snakes, alligators, egrets, migratory birds and other wildlife, often contain rare and threatened plant species. The sand rims and bays are thought to date back 30,000 to 100,000 years, their origins not really known. The road into the

Heritage Preserve just past the park gives the best look at the Carolina Bay with its unusual sand rim and dunes.

Little Pee Dee State Park is a scenic park although not a large one. At the end of the Park Access Road, stop at the park office for a map and information. Beside the park office is a cute "photo op" spot where visitors can take a memory picture. The day we visited one of the park rangers was planting trees outside the office and we enjoyed chatting with him and with staff and campers at the office. Little Pee Dee's property is centered around 54-acre Lake Norton. A paved pathway leads across from the park office to the lake through a scenic picnic area, with a lakeside pavilion, and a nice playground. In the middle of this area is a small square fence surrounding a stump of petrified wood and an informational plaque. This fossilized wood, found in Dillon Country, is estimated to be at least 10,000 years old.

Beyond this recreation area is a 75-foot pier/dock reaching out into the lake, a nice spot for lake fishing. Boating is allowed on the lake and there is a boat ramp nearby. Visitors

can bring their own boat or rent jon boats with an electric trolling motor, kayaks, or canoes. Little Pee Dee also has a swim beach area with a swim ramp. Fishing can be enjoyed not only on the lake but in the black waters of the Little Pee River at the southern end of the park boundary. Fish commonly caught include bream, bass, and catfish. From the fishing pier, be sure to walk along the shaded lake trail to the dam and spillway. A long bridge crosses the lake at this spot and you can walk over the bridge and wander for a short distance along the lakeside—also a good spot to bank fish.

For a longer walk, near the park office is the entrance to the park's 1.3-miles Beaver Pond Nature Trail, a quiet, peaceful woods trail easy for all ages and abilities. You can hike the shorter 0.7-miles in-and-out portion of the trail or the longer loop that reaches back to the edge of Lake Norton and the Carolina Bay area. At the back of the trail by a marshy pond is a wooden viewing platform with rest benches.

The campground area in this park lies along two scenic winding loop roads along the lake side. There are 50 campsites, 32 standard campsites for RVs with electric and water, but no sewer, and 18 campsites for

tents only. Within the campground are two restroom areas, one in Loop A and the other in Loop B, plus a waste disposal area and a dump station. All the campsites have picnic tables and many look out directly onto Lake Norton. Near the entrance to the campground on a loop road by the lake are two more picnic pavilions and many well-worn trails wander down to the lake here for fishing or wading. In the campground is also the park's one cabin for rent, small in size with no running water or a bathroom, but good for two to four to share with a fire pit and lake views. Although not a large park with many amenities, Little Pee Dee State Park is calm, picturesque, and relaxing, and popular with coastal travelers and many locals in the area.

Woods Bay State Park

Pee Dee - Florence County
Park Address: 11020 Woods Bay Road, Olanta, SC 29114
Park Size: 1550 acres   Month Visited: October
Directions: From Interstate 95, take Olanta exit onto Hwy 341.
Turn right after passing Mt. Zion Church onto County Road 43.
Follow to end of the road and turn right again on Woods Bay Road
and watch for park entrance on left.

Park Description:

Although covering a lot of acreage, Woods Bay is a small park tucked far away from towns in a rural area. It is best known for its large, undisturbed Carolina Bay, one of the few remaining of its size in the Mid-Atlantic coastal area. A smaller bay can also be found at Pee Dee State Park. A Carolina Bay is a boggy, lake-like depression in the earth, often oval-shaped and filled with shallow water. The origins of the bays, usually in a marsh-like jungle setting, are unknown but the bays provide a natural habitat for a diverse range of wildlife, often including rare and endangered animals and plants. More than 200 species of animals, including hundreds of bird species, live in the cypress-tupelo swamp and surrounding forest and marshland that comprises Woods Bay. You may spot herons, egrets, osprey, hawks, eagles and songbirds. You may also see turkeys, raccoons, otters, frogs, turtles, alligators, and possibly cottonmouth, rat snakes, and other water snakes. Woods Bay also has flowers in season and some unusual carnivorous plants. Wetlands insects are prevalent, too, like mosquitoes and yellow flies, which give a nasty, stinging bite, so be sure to bring bug repellent.

The road into Woods Bay ends at a small parking lot. Next to it is the park office, the only building in the park, which—when open—contains a Nature Center offering interesting area information and natural exhibits including a giant 14-foot alligator, known as Tex. Next to the office are restrooms and a large picnic pavilion with a grill. These are the park's only amenities except for its trails. There are no campgrounds or camping areas in this park.

Behind the park office the 0.75-miles Mill Pond Nature Trail circles around a swampy, wetland pond. Mill Pond has bream and bass and you can fish from the banks. The trail was once an old road through an area where two grist mills and a cotton gin used to be and as you walk by the dam area, you may spot where one of the old grist mills stood.

Woods Bay also has a canoe trail and many visitors bring their canoes or kayaks to paddle the one-mile Canoe Trail winding through a part of the bay. The canoe trail begins at a put-in point within the park and winds through the waters to a loop turn before returning. It takes about an hour to complete. The trail is well-marked and wildlife can be spotted along the way in the waters, darkened from the plant life within, and seen in the cypress swamp the route passes through.

A highlight for visitors to this park is the 1,150-foot Boardwalk Trail that winds through the cypress-tupelo swamp not far from the canoe trail. To get to the boardwalk, follow the signs a short distance beyond the pavilion to the boardwalk's beginning. This low, wooden boardwalk winds through the bay with informational plaques along the way to tell more about the area, its plants and wildlife. Visitors are likely to see alligators in the waters off the boardwalk, as many make their home here. Snakes, water birds, frogs, salamanders, and turtles sunning on an old log may also be spotted, too. In the late afternoon and early evening you may also hear a symphony of frog sounds, as Carolina Bays are wonderful frog habitats.

Lee State Park

Pee Dee - Lee County
Park Address: 2400 Park Access Road, Dillon, SC 29538
Park Size: 2839 acres   Month Visited: October
Directions: From Interstate 20, about midway between Colum-
bia and Florence, take Exit 123 and turn north on Lee State Park
Road. Go one mile and turn left into park entrance.

Park Description:

Easy to access right off Interstate 20, Lee State Park, named for Confederate General Robert E. Lee, is a wonderful spot you won't want to miss visiting.
Clean and neat, it offers a diversity of sights to see—with scenic picnic areas, a
multitude of hiking, biking, and equestrian trails, unique artesian wells, a fine
campground, lovely lakes, ponds, and wetlands, and the Lynches River for paddlers and anglers. Lee's entry road leads directly to the middle of the park grounds
and to a parking area by the office and visitor center, the perfect place to start your
exploration. Inside the center you can pick up maps, informational brochures, and
browse through a gift shop and Education Center.

Around the grounds near the office is a wide tree-shaded area with picnic
tables tucked under the trees, where we stopped to eat our lunch, and two beautiful picnic pavilions. Both pavilions were built in the 1930s by the Civilian Conservation Corps (CCC) when Lee State Park was created, and you will see other
historic structures around the park showcasing the CCC's unique workmanship

and building skills. For more information about the CCC, be sure to ask for a CCC history brochure at the park office along with a bird guide. Lee has 144 species of birds and you may see and hear many of these at your visit, especially around the park's lakes, wetland ponds and along the river.

Behind the pavilions a paved trail winds into the woods to a Wetland Boardwalk Trail, a short half-mile trail winding into a wetlands swamp area. Here you may spot water birds, dragonflies, turtles, and other wildlife in the ponds. Along the way are informational kiosks and waysides telling you more about the natural area you're walking through. The trail ends at an observation point in the pond with benches for a rest if you want to pause before turning around to head back. This boardwalk trail wasn't written up on the park site but we are pleased we found it.

For more easy hiking fun we headed next behind the picnic area to pick up a portion of the Floodplain Foot Trail. This approximately 1-mile trail section travels by a pond and across a scenic rock bridge and sandstone spillway, constructed by the CCC, to wind around the perimeter of Artesian Lake. Along the lakeside are picnic tables and spots to rest and enjoy this pretty lake. In summer an area of the lake is roped off for swimming. At the back of the lake are two of the park's artesian wells. This South Carolina area, geologically, has a band of confined aquifers below ground under a deep stratum of rock, sand and gravel. When the CCC drilled below that

stratum to the water confined under pressure, it pushed the water to the surface in artesian wells. In total, the CCC drilled seven artesian wells in the 1930s, to bring clear, cold drinking water to the surface, and, fortunately, four of these still exist in the park. The well water also feeds the Artesian Lake, and if you wade into the swim area in summer, the water below the warmer surface is chilly and cold.

East of the lake, picnic area, and park office is the park's campground. The campground, winding around a figure-eight road, has 48 campsites, 25 standard sites and 23 sites for equestrian camping. All 48 campsites have water and electric, a comfort station and dump station. Lots are flat and tree-shaded with picnic tables and grills. Campers love this park, and it is especially a delight to equestrians with designated equestrian campsite corrals, a ten-stall barn, a show ring and 12 miles of riding trails.

Before you leave the camp section of the park, look for the Sandhills Trail across from the campground. Even though it's only a half-mile in length don't miss it because it is lined with cute Harry Potter Houses tacked on trees along the way—an unexpected treat!

Next, following the Loop Road guide that we picked up at the park office, we moved on to explore the pretty five mile sandy road that circles around through the woods and back in the park. The scenic drive travels past trail entrances and the horse stall and show ring area before looping to follow along the

Lynches River and back to the park office area. We passed bikers, walkers, and horseback riders enjoying the road, and at about two miles, we stopped to check out the primitive youth camp area. Organized groups up to 75 can stay here and we especially enjoyed finding another artesian well and pool here and exploring the historic CCC cabin beside it. Originally the CCC built five cabins at Lee State Park but this is the only one now remaining.

Beyond the camp, the road winds around to travel along the Lynches River. Canoe and kayak enthusiasts love to paddle this section of the river and anglers enjoy fishing along the banks, catching redbreast, bass, bream and other fish. Although there are no specific put-in points in the park, boaters can find several ramps near the park for good access. At four miles along the river, watch for the fourth of the park's artesian wells near Mulberry Island. A side road also leads to an area where fishing cabins once stood, but we missed seeing much of this area due to flooding at our visit, often occurring as this section of the road runs through a floodplain. The Lynches River, the longest river in the state and designated as a State Scenic River, is named for Thomas Lynch, a signer of the Declaration, and the river winds for 111 miles from upper South Carolina almost to the coast.

ALPHABETICAL STATE PARK INDEX

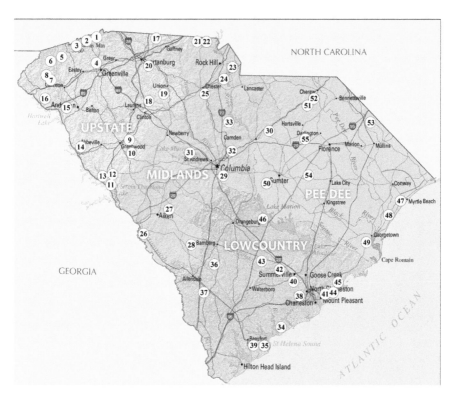

UPSTATE PARKS
1 Jones Gap State Park
2 Caesars Head State Park
3 Table Rock State Park
4 Paris Mountain State Park
5 Keowee-Toxaway State Park
6 Devil's Fork State Park
7 Oconee Station State Historic Site
8 Oconee State Park
9 Lake Greenwood State Park
10 Ninety Six National Historic Site
11 Hamilton Branch State Park
12 Baker Creek State Park
13 Hickory Knob State Park
14 Calhoun Falls State Park
15 Sadlers Creek State Park
16 Lake Hartwell State Park
17 Cowpens National Battlefield Park
18 Battle of Musgrove Mill State Historic Park
19 Rose Hill Plantation State Historic Site
20 Croft State Park

PEE DEE PARKS
47 Myrtle Beach State Park
48 Huntington Beach State Park
49 Hampton Plantation State Historic Site
50 Poinsett State Park
51 H Cooper Black State Park
52 Cheraw State Park
53 Little Pee Dee State Park
54 Woods Bay State Park
55 Lee State Park

MIDLANDS PARKS
21 Kings Mountain National Military Park
22 Kings Mountain State Park
23 Andrew Jackson State Park
24 Landsford Canal State Park
25 Chester State Park
26 Redcliffe Plantation State Historic Site
27 Aiken State Park
28 Barnwell State Park
29 Congaree National Park
30 Goodale State Park
31 Dreher Island State Park
32 Sesquicentennial State Park
33 Lake Wateree State Park

LOWCOUNTRY PARKS
34 Edisto Beach State Park
35 Hunting Island State Park
36 Rivers Bridge State Park
37 Lake Warren State Park
38 Charles Towne Landing State Park
39 Reconstruction Era National Historic Park
40 Colonial Dorchester State Historic Park
41 Fort Sumter National Monument
42 Givhans Ferry State Park
43 Colleton State Park
44 Fort Moultrie National Historic Park
45 Charles Pinckney National Historic Site
46 Santee State Park

About The Authors

J.L. and Lin Stepp are the co-authors of *Exploring South Carolina State Parks.*

Lin Stepp is a *New York Times* and *USA Today* Best-Selling international author. A businesswoman and educator, she was on faculty at Tusculum College teaching research and psychology for 20 years, worked in marketing, sales, production art, and regional publishing for over 25 years, and has editorial and writing experience in regional magazines and in the academic field. Stepp writes engaging, heart-warming contemporary Southern fiction with a strong sense of place and has eighteen published novels, each set in different locations around the Smoky Mountains. Her past titles include twelve novels in the Smoky Mountain series, three South Carolina coastal novels in the Edisto Trilogy, and two titles in the new Mountain Home book series, the latest of which are *Happy Valley* (2020) and *Downsizing* (2021). In addition she had a novella published in Kensington Publishing's *When the Snow Falls* Christmas anthology and with her husband has co-authored a Smoky Mountains hiking guidebook and two state park guidebooks. For more about her work see: www.linstepp.com

J.L. Stepp is the co-author of the best-selling Smoky Mountain hiking guidebook titled *The Afternoon Hiker* and he and his wife Lin have also co-authored two state park guidebooks *Discovering Tennessee State Parks* (2018) and *Exploring South Carolina State Parks* (2021). Stepp enjoys a wide variety of outdoor sports, including golf, fishing, and hiking. His background includes over 45 years in sales, marketing, management, and publications. A native East Tennessean and graduate of The University of Tennessee, Stepp owns S & S Communications, established in 1990, which publishes a monthly outdoor magazine called *Tennessee Fishing & Hunting Guide,* covering fishing and hunting topics in Tennessee and distributed monthly in print form to advertisers and online at: www.tnfhg.com. He and his wife Lin travel widely around the southeast region signing at bookstores and festivals and speaking for organizations and events. Contact at: steppcom@aol.com